Two Orations of the Emperor Julian

One to the Sovereign Sun and the other to the Mother of the Gods

By

Flavius Claudius Iulianus

Translated from the Latin by

Thomas Taylor

First published in 1793

Published by Left of Brain Books

Copyright © 2023 Left of Brain Books

ISBN 978-1-396-32650-9

First Edition

All rights reserved. No part of this publication may be reproduced, distributed, or transmitted in any form or by any means, including photocopying, recording, or other electronic or mechanical methods, without the prior written permission of the publisher, except in the case of brief quotations permitted by copyright law. Left of Brain Books is a division of Left Of Brain Onboarding Pty Ltd.

PUBLISHER'S PREFACE

About the Book

"This translation of two works on pagan theology with a Platonic theme by the Roman Emperor Julian is extremely rare. It was originally published in 1793, and reprinted in 1932 in an edition of 500 copies, one of which we used as the basis for this etext. (The 1932 edition had no copyright notice).

The short-lived Emperor Julian (331-363 CE) suceeded Constantius in 361 CE. He shocked the empire by renouncing Christianity, which earned him the title 'the Apostate' by Church historians. He issued an edict of religious freedom, rebuilt the Pagan temples, ended banishment of religious exiles, and eliminated special privileges for Christian officials. He founded the Neo-platonic school of philosophy. Julian spurned the decadant Byzantine palace; he dressed simply, studied philosophy, promulgated tax reform, and fostered study of the humanities and arts. However, his reign lasted only twenty months; he died in June of 363 in battle with the Persians, possibly at the hand of a Christian.

This book is as notable for its author as for its translator. Thomas Taylor (1758-1835) was a prolific classicist and one of the first modern neo-Platonists. Although he was deprecated while alive, he had a huge influence on H.P. Blatavsky and other theosophists."

(Quote from sacred-texts.com)

About the Author

Flavius Claudius Iulianus (331 - 363)

"Flavius Claudius Iulianus (331–June 26, 363), was a Roman Emperor (361–363) of the Constantinian dynasty. He was the last pagan Roman Emperor, and tried to promote the Roman religious traditions of earlier centuries as a means of slowing the spread of Christianity.

His philosophical studies earned him the attribute the Philosopher during the period of his life and of those of his successors. Christian sources commonly refer to him as Julian the Apostate, because of his rejection of Christianity, conversion to Theurgy (a late form of Neoplatonism), and attempt to rid the empire of Christianity while bringing back ancient Roman religion. He is also sometimes referred to as Julian II, to distinguish him from Didius Julianus."

(Quote from top40-charts.com)

CONTENTS

PUBLISHER'S PREFACE
INTRODUCTION 1
   TO APOLLO AND THE SUN 17
   THE EMPEROR JULIAN'S ORATION TO THE SOVEREIGN SUN 22
   THE EMPEROR JULIAN'S ORATION TO THE MOTHER OF THE GODS 53
   TO THE ANCIENT PLATONIC PHILOSOPHERS 77
ENDNOTES 78

INTRODUCTION

THE Emperor Julian, the author of the two following Orations, is well known in the character of a Sovereign and an Apostate which he once sustained, but very few are acquainted with him in the characters of a Theologist and Philosopher, which he displays through the whole of his works, in a manner by no means contemptible or weak. It is true, indeed, that his philosophical and theological attainments are not to be compared with those of Pythagoras, Plato, and Proclus, who appear to have arrived at the summit of human piety and wisdom, or with those of many of the Platonists prior and posterior to Proclus; but, at the same time, they were certainly far superior to those which many celebrated antients possessed, or which even fell to the share of such a man as the biographer Plutarch.

Indeed it is impossible that a man burthened with the weight of a corrupt empire, such as that of Rome, or that the governor of any community except a republic, like that of Plato, should be able to philosophize in the most exquisite degree, and leave monuments behind him of perfect erudition and science. Julian, however, appears to have possessed as much of the philosophical genius as could possibly be the portion of an Emperor of Rome, and was doubtless as much superior to any other Emperor, either prior or posterior to him, as the philosophy and theology which he zealously professed transcend all others in dignity and worth. Hence, in the ensuing orations, he has happily blended the majestic diction of a Roman Emperor with the gravity of sentiment peculiar to a Platonic philosopher, and with that scientific and manly piety which is so conspicuous in the writings of antient theologists. His language is, indeed, highly magnificent, and in every respect becoming the exalted rank which he sustained, and the great importance of the subjects of his discourse: in short, the grandeur of his soul is so visible in his composition, that we may safely credit what he asserted of himself, that he was formerly Alexander the Great. And if we consider the actions of Alexander and Julian, we shall easily be induced to believe, that it was one and the same person who, in different periods, induced the Indians, Bactrians, and inhabitants of Caucasus, to worship the Grecian deities: took down the contemptible ensign of his predecessor, and raised in its stead the majestic Roman eagles; and every where endeavoured to restore a religion which is coeval with the universe, by banishing gigantically-daring, and barbaric belief.

The first of these orations, which celebrates that glorious divinity, the Sun, is not only valuable for the piety and eloquence displayed in its composition, but for its containing much important information from a treatise of Jamblichus on the gods, which is unfortunately lost. The name of Jamblichus must, indeed, be dear to every genuine lover of Platonism, and any work replete with his doctrines may certainly, with justice, lay claim to immortality. However, as the theology of Orpheus, Pythagoras, and Plato, does not appear to have been unfolded in the most consummate perfection, even by Jamblichus himself, this great talk being reserved for the incomparable Proclus, we shall find in such books of Proclus as are fortunately preserved, a more accurate account in some particulars of the essence and powers of the Sun. This account I shall lay before the reader, (after I have premised a few particulars concerning the existence and nature of the gods), that he may see in what the Emperor's discourse is defective, and in what it is agreeable to the truth.

That after the first cause, then, who, from the transcendent excellence of his nature, was justly considered by all the, pious antients as superessential and ineffable, there should be a divine multitude, or, in other words, gods subordinate indeed to the first, but at the same time exquisitely allied to him, is a doctrine so congenial with the unperverted conceptions of the soul, that it can only be rejected during the most degraded generations of mankind: for if there be no such thing as a vacuum either in incorporeal or corporeal natures, and if in every well-ordered progression the similar precedes the dissimilar, and this, so as to cause the whole series to be united in the most perfect degree, it is necessary that the first progeny of the first god should be no other than gods. [1]

Indeed, those who are skilled in the most scientific dialectic of Plato, know that a unity or monad is every where the leader of a kindred multitude; and that, in consequence of this, there is one first nature and many natures, one first soul and many souls, one first intellect and many intellects, and one first god and a kindred multitude of gods.

But as this highest god, from the transcendent simplicity of his nature, was profoundly called by the Platonic philosophers the one, hence all the gods, considered according to the characteristics or summits of their natures, will be unities; but they will differ from the first cause in this, that he is alone superessential without any addition, and is perfectly exempt from all habitude or alliance to any other nature, whereas each of the other gods is participated by something inferior to itself, viz. either by being, life, intellect, soul, or body, from which participations all the divine orders are produced, and through which they become subordinate to the highest god.

In addition, therefore, to what I have said concerning the first cause, and the gods, his immediate progeny, in my Introduction to Plato's Parmenides, the following observations, extracted from the 6th book of Proclus, on that most theological dialogue, will, I doubt not, be highly acceptable to the truly liberal reader. "The one, then, is the principle of all things, since to be united is to every thing good, and the greatest of goods; but that which is every way separated from unity is evil, and the greatest of evils; since it becomes the cause of dissimilitude, privation of sympathy, division, and a departure from a subsistence according to nature. The first cause, therefore, as supplying all things with the greatest good, unites all things, and is, on this account, called the one. And hence the gods, from their surpassing similitude to the first god, will be unities proceeding from this one principle, and yet ineffably absorbed in his nature. Thus, for instance, (that we may illustrate this doctrine by an example) we perceive many causes of light, some of which are celestial and others sublunary; for light proceeds to our terrestrial abode from material fire, from the moon, and from the other stars, and this, so as to be different according to the difference of its cause. But if we explore the one monad of all mundane light, from which other lucid natures and sources of light derive their subsistence, we shall find that it is no other, than the apparent orb of the Sun; for this orbicular body proceeds, as it is said, from. an occult and supermundane order, and disseminates in all mundane natures a light commensurate with each."

"Shall we say then that this apparent body is the principle of light? But this is endued with interval, and is divisible, and light proceeds from the different parts which it contains. But we are at present investigating the one principle of light: shall we say, therefore, that the ruling soul of this body generates mundane light? This indeed produces light, but not primarily, for it is itself multitude; and light contains a representation of a simple and uniform subsistence. May not intellect therefore, which is the cause of soul, be the fountain of this light! Intellect, indeed, is more united than soul, but is not that which is properly and primarily the principle of light. It remains, therefore, that the one of this intellect, its summit, and, as it were, flower, must be the first principle of mundane light. For this is properly the sun which reigns over the visible place, and, according to Plato in the Republic, is the offspring of the good; since every unity proceeds from thence, and every deity is the progeny of the unity of unities, and the fountain of the gods. And as the good is the principle of light to intelligibles, in like manner the unity of the solar order is the principle of light to all visible natures, and is analogous to the good, in which it is occultly established, and from which it never departs."

"But this unity having an order prior to the solar intellect, there is also in intellect, so far as intellect, a unity participated from this unity, which is emitted into it like a seed, and through which intellect is united with the unity or deity of the sun. This, too, is the case with the soul of the sun; for this, through the one which she contains, is elevated through the one of intellect as a medium, to the deity of the sun. And we must understand the same with respect to the body of the sun, that there is in this a certain resounding echo, as it were, of the primary solar one: for it is necessary that the solar body should participate of things superior to itself; of soul, according to the life which is disseminated in it; of intellect, according to its form; and of unity, according to its one, since soul participates both of intellect and this one, and participations are different from the things which are participated. You may say, therefore, that the proximate cause of the solar light is this unity of the solar orb."

"In like manner, if we should investigate the root, as it were, of all bodies, from which celestial and sublunary bodies, wholes and parts, blossom into existence, we may not improperly say that this is Nature, which is the principle of motion and rest to all bodies, and which is established in them, whether they are in motion or at rest. But I mean by Nature, the one life of the world, which, being subordinate to intellect and soul, participates through these of generation. And this, indeed, is more a principle than many and partial natures, but is not that which is properly the principle of bodies; for this contains a multitude of powers, and through such as are different, governs different parts of the universe: but we are now investigating the one and common principle of all bodies, and not many and distributed principles. If, therefore, we wish to discover this one principle, we must raise ourselves to that which is most united in Nature to its flower, and that through which it is a deity, by which it is suspended from its proper fountain, connects, unites, and causes the universe to have a sympathetic consent with itself. This one, therefore, is the principle of all generation) and is that which reigns over the many powers of Nature, over partial natures, and universally over every thing subject to the dominion of Nature."

Thus far Proclus, from which admirable passage it is easy to infer that principles are every where unities, and that the highest principles are no other than gods or superessential blossoms, involved in unproceeding union with the first god, and absorbed in ineffable light. But the same incomparable man farther observes, "All these unities are in each other, and are profoundly united with each other, and their union is far greater than the communion and sameness which subsist in beings; for in these there is, indeed, a mutual mixture of forms, similitude and friendship, and a participation of each other; but the union of the gods, as being a union of unities, is much more uniform, ineffable, and transcendent: for here all are in all which does not take place in forms or ideas; [2] and their unmingled purity, and the characteristic of each, in a manner far surpassing the diversity in ideas, preserves their natures unconfused, and distinguishes their peculiar powers. Hence some of them are more universal, and others more particular; some of them are characterized according to abiding, others according to progression, and others according to conversion; some again are generative, others reductive, and others demiurgic; and universally there are different characteristics of different gods, viz. the connective, perfective, demiurgic assimilative, and such others as are celebrated posterior to these: so that all are in all, and yet each is, at the same time, separate and distinct."

"Indeed, we obtain this knowledge of their union and characteristics from the natures by which they are participated; for, with respect to the apparent gods, we say, that there is one soul of the sun and another of the earth directing our attention to the apparent bodies of these divinities, which possess much variety in their essence, powers, and dignity among wholes. As, therefore, we apprehend the difference of incorporeal essences from sensible inspection, in like manner from the variety of incorporeal essences we are enabled to know something of the unmingled distinction of the first and superessential unities, and of the characteristics of each; for each unity has a multitude suspended from its nature, which is either intelligible [3] alone, or, at the same time, intelligible and intellectual, or intellectual alone; and this last is either participated or not participated, and this again is either supermundane or mundane: and thus far does the progression of the unities extend." And, shortly after, he adds, "As trees by their extremities are rooted in the earth, and through this are earthly in every part, in the same manner divine natures are rooted by their summits in the one, and each is a unity and one, through its unconfused union with the one itself."

If the reader, therefore, unites these beautiful passages with what I have delivered concerning the gods, in my Introduction to the Parmenides, and has, at the same time, a genius adapted to such speculations, he will find that the observation of Jamblichus is no less admirable than true, "that a knowledge of the Gods is virtue, wisdom, and consummate felicity, and assimilates us to the Gods themselves." He will find that the theology of Plato is the progeny of the most consummate science and wisdom, and that it is as much superior to all other theological systems which oppose it, as reality to fiction, or intellect to irrational opinion.

Having premised thus much, I shall now present the reader with an account of the nature of the Sun, extracted from Proclus on Plato's Theology, from his Commentaries on the Timæus, and from his Scholia on the Cratylus, in which he will find the most arcane and perfect information concerning this mighty divinity which can perhaps at present be obtained. [4]

The fontal sun, then, subsists in Jupiter, the perfect artificer of the world, who produced the hypostasis of, the sun from his own essence. Through the solar fountain contained in his essence, the Demiurgus generates solar powers in the principles of the universe, and a triad of solar gods, through which all things are unfolded into light, and are perfected and replenished with intellectual goods; through the first of these solar monads participating unpolluted light and intelligible harmony; but from the other two, efficacious power, vigour, and demiurgic perfection. The sun subsists in the most beautiful proportion to the good: for as the splendour proceeding from the good is the light of intelligible natures; so that proceeding from Apollo is the light of the intellectual world; and that which emanates from the apparent sun is the light of the sensible world. And both the sun and Apollo are analogous to the good; but sensible light and intellectual truth are analogous to superessential light. But though Apollo and the sun subsist in wonderful union with each other, yet they likewise inherit a proper distinction and diversity of nature. Hence, by poets inspired by Phœbus, the different generative causes of the two are celebrated, and the fountains are distinguished from which their hypostasis is derived. At the same time they are described as closely united with each other, and are celebrated with each other's mutual appellations: for the sun vehemently rejoices to be celebrated as Apollo; and Apollo, when he is invoked as the sun, benignantly imparts the splendid light of truth. It is the illustrious property of Apollo to collect multitude into one, to comprehend number in one, and from one to produce many natures; to convolve in himself, through intellectual simplicity, all the variety of secondary natures; and, through one hyparxis, to collect into one multiform essences and powers. This god, through a simplicity exempt from multitude, imparts to secondary natures prophetic truth; for that which is simple is the same with. that which is true: but through his liberated essence he imparts a purifying, unpolluted, and preserving power: and his emission of arrows is the symbol of his destroying every thing inordinate, wandering, and immoderate in the world. But his revolution is the symbol of the harmonic motion of the universe, collecting all things into union and consent. And these four powers of the god may be accommodated to the three solar monads, which he contains. The first monad [5], therefore, of this god is enunciative of truth, and of the intellectual light which subsists occultly in the gods. But the second [6] is destructive of every thing wandering and confused: but the third [7] causes all things to subsist in symmetry and familiarity with each other, through harmonic reasons. And the unpolluted and most pure cause, which he comprehends in himself, obtains the principality, illuminating all things with perfection and power, according to nature, and banishing every thing contrary to these.

Hence, of the solar triad, the first monad unfolds intellectual light, enunciates it to all secondary natures, fills all things with universal truth, and converts them to the intellect of the gods; which employment is ascribed to the prophetic power of Apollo, who produces into light the truth contained ill divine natures, and perfects that which is unknown in the secondary orders of things. But the second and third monads are the causes of efficacious vigour, demiurgic effection in the universe, and perfect energy, according to which these monads adorn every sensible nature, and exterminate every thing indefinite and inordinate in the world.

And one monad is analogous to musical fabrication, and to the harmonic providence of natures which are moved. But the second is analogous to that which is destructive of all confusion, and of that perturbation which is contrary to form, and the orderly disposition of the universe. But the third monad, which supplies all things with an abundant communion of beauty, and extends true beautitude to all things, bounds the solar principles, and guards its triple progression. In a similar manner, likewise, it illuminates progressions with a perfect and intellectual measure of a blessed life, by those purifying and pæonian powers of the king Apollo, which obtain an analogous principality in the sun.--The sun is allotted a supermundane [8] order in the world, an unbegotten supremacy among generated forms, and an intellectual dignity among sensible natures. Hence he has a twofold progression, one in conjunction with the other mundane gods, but the other exempt from them, supernatural and unknown. For the Demiurgus, according to Plato in the Timæus, enkindled in the solar sphere a light unlike the splendour of the other planets, producing it from his own essence, extending to mundane natures, as it were from certain secret recesses, a symbol of intellectual essences, and exhibiting to the universe the arcane nature of the supermundane gods.

Hence, when the sun first arose, he astonished the mundane gods, all of whom were desirous of dancing round him, and of being replenished with his light. The sun, too, governs the twofold co-ordinations of the world, which co-ordinations are denominated hands, by those who are skilled in divine concerns, because they are effective, motive, and demiurgic of the universe. But they are considered as twofold; one the right hand, but the other the left.

And lastly, the sun being supermundane, emits the fountains of light; for among supermundane natures there is a solar world and total light; and this light is a monad prior to the empyrean, ætherial, and material worlds [9]. And thus much for an account of the sun, from Proclus, On the Timæus and Theology of Plato: the following is from his Scholia on the Cratylus.

In the first place, then, Proclus informs us, that there is a great correspondence between the Coric series, or the order belonging to Proserpine, and the Apolloniacal; for the former is the unity of the middle triad of Rulers, (meaning of the supermundane gods) and emits from herself vivific powers; but the latter converts the solar principles to one union: and the solar principles are allotted a subsistence immediately after the vivific. Hence (says he) according to Orpheus, when Ceres delivered up the government to Proserpine, she thus admonished her:

Αυταρ Απολλωνος θαλερον λεχος εισαναβασα,
Τεξεται αγλαα τεκνα πυριφλεγεθοντα προσωποις.

That is,

But next Apollo's florid bed ascend;
For thus the god fam'd offspring shall beget,

Refulgent with the beams of glowing fire.

But how could this be the case, unless there was a considerable degree of communion between these divinities.

But it is requisite to know thus much concerning Apollo, that, according to the first and most natural conception, his name signifies the cause of union, and that power which collects multitude into one; and this mode of speculation concerning his name harmonizes with all the orders of the god. After this, he observes, in answer to the question why Socrates, in the Cratylus, begins from the medicinal power of the gods, proceeds through his prophetic and arrow-darting powers, and lastly ends in his harmonic power, that all the energies of this divinity subsist in all the orders of beings, but that different energies appear to have more or less dominion in different orders: thus, for instance, the medicinal power of Apollo is most apparent in the sublunary region, for

There slaughter, rage, and countless Ills beside,
Disease, decay, and rottenness reside. [10]

And as these are moved in an inordinate manner, they require to be restored from a condition contrary, into one agreeable to nature, and from incommensuration and manifold division, into symmetry and union.

But the prophetic energy of the god is most apparent in the heavens; for there his enunciative power shines forth, unfolding intelligible goods to celestial natures, and on this account he revolves together with the sun, with whom he participates the same intellect in common; since the sun also illuminates whatever heaven contains, and extends a unifying power to all its parts. But his arrow-darting energy mostly prevails among the liberated [11] gods; for there ruling over the wholes [12] which the universe contains, he excites their motions by his rays, which are always assimilated to arrows, extirpates every thing inordinate, and fills all things with demiurgic gifts. And though he has a separate and exempt subsistence, he reaches all things by his energies.

Again, his harmonic power is more predominant in the ruling supermundane order; for it is this divinity who harmonizing the universe, establishes about himself according to one union the choir of the Muses, and produces by this means, as a certain Theurgist says, "the harmony of exulting light." Apollo, therefore, as we have shewn, is harmonic, and this is likewise the case with the other Apollos [13] which are contained in the earth, and the other spheres; but this power appears in some places more and in others less. These powers too, subsist in the god himself in an united manner, and exempt from other natures, but in those attendants of the gods who are superior to us, divisibly and according to participation; for there is a great multitude of medicinal, prophetic, harmonic, and arrow-darting angels, dæmons, and heroes, suspended from Apollo, who distribute in a partial manner the uniform powers of the god.

But it is necessary to consider each of these powers according to one definite characteristic; as, for instance, his harmonic power, according to its binding together separated multitude; his prophetic power, according to the enunciative; his arrow-darting power, according to its being subvertive of an inordinate nature; and his medicinal power, according to its perfective energy. We should likewise speculate these characteristics differently in gods, angels, dæmons, heroes, men, animals, and plants; for the powers of the gods extend from on high to the last of things, and at the same time appear in an accommodated manner in each; and the Telestic or mystic art endeavours through sympathy to conjoin these ultimate participants with the gods. But in all these orders we must carefully observe, that this god is the cause of union to multiplied natures: for his medicinal power, which takes away the multiform nature of disease, imparts uniform health; since health is symmetry, and a subsistence according to nature, but that which is contrary to nature is multifarious. Thus too, his prophetic power, which unfolds the simplicity of truth, takes away the variety of that which is false; but his arrow-darting power, which exterminates every thing furious and wild, but prepares that which is orderly and gentle to exercise dominion, vindicates to itself unity, and exterminates a disordered nature tending to multitude: and his musical power, through rythm and harmony, places a bond, friendship and union in wholes, and subdues the contraries of these.

And all these powers, indeed, subsist primarily in an exempt manner and uniformly in the demiurgus [14] of wholes, but secondarily and separately in Apollo. Hence Apollo is not the same with the demiurgic intellect; for this comprehends these powers totally and paternally, but Apollo, with subjection, imitating his father; since all the energies and powers of secondary gods, are comprehended in the Demiurgus according to cause. And the Demiurgus fabricates and adorns the universe according to all these powers, and in a collected manner; but the other deities which proceed from him, co-operate with their father according to different powers.

Thus far the truly admirable Proclus, who certainly merited the appellation of Coryphæus which is given him by Damascius, in the most eminent degree; for he was beyond all doubt the man who, in the language of Ammonius Hermeas [15], possessed the ability of interpreting the doctrines of the ancients, and a scientific judgment of the nature of things, in the greatest perfection possible to man. For my own part, indeed, the whole of time would not be sufficient to pay him thanks adequate to the benefits which I have received from his incomparable works; and I shall consider the employment (if permitted me) of translating and illustrating the whole of his philosophical works in English, as forming a very principal part of the felicity of my life. I only add farther concerning this Oration to the Sun, that it is addressed to one) Sallust, who was a governor of some Roman province, who appears to have been greatly esteemed by the Emperor, and who of course was a professor of the genuine religion of mankind.

With respect to the Oration to the Mother of the Gods, it is necessary to observe, that this divinity first subsists at the summit of that order of gods which is called by the Chaldean theologists νοητος και νεορος, i.e. intelligible, and at the same time intellectual; that she is there no other than the celebrated goddess Night; and that she produces from thence, in the intellectual order, Rhea, Ceres, Tethys and Juno, each of whom, from subsisting according to the same characteristic, is the mother of all the divinities respectively subordinate to each. So that this vivific series, or luminous chain, commences from the occult goddess Night, and extends to the utmost extremities of animated being. Indeed, the various orders of the gods are in reality no other than the golden chain of Homer [16], the topmost link of which is suspended, from the ineffable principle of all things, and whose series is terminated only by the dark, fluctuating, and rebounding receptacle of matter.

I shall only observe farther at present, that the Emperor's explanation of the mystic fable, respecting Attis and the Mother of the Gods is agreeable to that of the philosopher Sallust, in his treatise On the Gods and the World, as may be seen in Chap. IV. of my translation of that invaluable work. I shall therefore conclude this Introduction with a hymn to Apollo and the Sun, considered as in a certain respect one and the same divinity, and in which the reader will find an epitome of a great part, of the arcane information concerning this mighty deity which has been already delivered.

TO APOLLO AND THE SUN [17]

The Sun's resplendent deity I sing,
The beauteous offspring of almighty Jove,
Who, thro' the vivifying solar fount
Within his fabricative mind conceal'd,
A triad form'd of splendid solar gods;
From whence the world's all-various forms emerg'd
From mystic darkness into beauteous light,
Perfect, and full of intellectual goods.
Hail! Supermundane king of light divine,
And fairest image of the unknown good:
For, as the light proceeding from the one,
The god of gods, and beauty's matchless flower,
Intelligibles, with deific rays
Occult, illumes; so from Apollo's beams
Exulting glorious through harmonic power,
The mental world with elevating light
Is fill'd exub'rant: and th' apparent Sun
Largely diffuses thro' the world of sense,
Light, all-prolific, beautiful, divine.
To thee, as bright Apollo, it belongs
All multitude in union to collect,
And many natures generate from one;
With vigour in thy essence to convolve
The diff'rent ranks of secondary forms;
And thro' one fair hyparxis [18] to combine

All-various essences and fertile powers.
'Tis thine, from multitude exempt, t' inspire
In forms subordinate, prophetic truth;

For truth and pure simplicity are one:
And of preserving unpolluted power,
Thy liberated essence is the source.
Fam'd mystic bards of old, in sacred song,
By thee inspir'd, as th' arrow-darting god,
Constant invok'd thee, with resistless sway,
Because thy vig'rous beams like arrows pierce,
And totally, whate'er of measure void the world
Inordinate or dark contains, destroy.
And last, thy revolution is the sign
Of motion, harmonizing into one
The various natures of this mighty whole.
Thy first bright Monad [19] hence, illustrious god,
Enunciates truth and intellectual light;
That light, which in the essence of the gods,
Subsists with rays uniting and unknown.
Thy second [20], ev'ry thing confus'd destroys:
And from thy third [21], the universe is bound
In beauteous symmetry and just consent,
Thro' splendid reasons and harmonic power.
Add, that thy essence, 'midst the mundane gods,
A super-mundane order is assign'd;
An unbegotten and supreme command
O'er all the ranks of generated forms;
And In the ever-flowing realms of sense,
An intellectual dignity of sway.
Progression two-fold, hence, to thee belongs,--
One in conjunction with the mundane gods,
The other supernat'ral and unknown:
For when the Demiurgus form'd the world,
He kindled in the solar sphere a light,
Unlike the splendour of the other orbs,
Drawn from his nature's most occult retreats,
A symbol fair of intellectual forms;
And openly announcing as it shines

To ev'ry part of this amazing whole,
The essence solitary and arcane

Of all the ruling, supermundane gods.
Hence too, when first thy beams the world adorn'd
The mundane gods were ravish'd at the sight;
And round thy orb, with emulative zeal
And symphony divine, desir'd to dance,
And draw abundant from thy fontal light.
'Tie thine by heat apparent to exalt
Corporeal natures from the sluggish earth,
Inspiring vivid, vegetative power;
And by a nature secretly divine,
And from the base alloy of matter free,
Inherent in thy all-productive rays,
Thou draw'st to union with thy wond'rous form,
Exalted souls, that In dark Hyle's realms
Indignant struggle for the courts of. light:
All beauteous, seven-rayed, supermundane god!
Whose mystic essence secretly emits
The splendid fountains of celestial light.
For 'midst the ruling, super-mundane gods
A solar world, and total light subsists;
A light, which as a fertile monad shines
Superior to the three corporeal worlds.
By sacred Oracles of old, 'tie said,
Thy glorious orb beyond the starry sphere
And in the last etherial world revolves.
But in thy course, harmoniously divine,
Thy orb, quadruply intersects these worlds;
And then twelve powers of radiant gods displays,
Thro' twelve divisions of the zone oblique.
And still abundant in productive might,
Each into three of diff'rent ranks divides.

Hence, from the fourfold elegance and grace
Of times and seasons, by thy course produc'd,
Mankind a triple benefit receive,
The circling Graces' never-failing gift.
All-bounteous god, by whom the soul is freed
Prom Generation's dark corporeal bands,
Assist THY OFFSPRING, borne on mental wings,
Beyond the reach of guileful Nature's hands
Swift to ascend, and gain thy beauteous world.
The subtle vestment of my soul refine,
Etherial, firm, and full of sacred light,
Her ancient vehicle by thee assign'd;
In which invelop'd, thro' the starry orbs,
Urg'd' by the Impulse of insane desire,

She fail'd precipitate, till Lethe's shore,
Involv'd in night, unhappily she touch'd,
And lost all knowledge of her pristine state:
O best of gods, blest dæmon crown'd with fire,
My soul's sure refuge in the hour of woe,
My port paternal in the courts of light,
Hear, and from punishment my soul absolve,
The punishment incurr'd by pristine guilt,
Thro' Lethe's darkness and terrene desire:
And if for long-extended years I'm doom'd
In these drear realms Heav'n's exile to remain,
Oh! grant me soon the necessary means
To gain that good which solitude confers
On souls emerging from the bitter waves
Of fraudful Hyle's black, impetuous flood.
That thus retiring from the vulgar herd,
And impious converse of the present age,
My soul may triumph o'er her natal ills;
And oft with thee In blissful union join'd
Thro' energy Ineffable, may soar

Beyond the highest super-mundane forms;
And in the vestibule supreme survey,
Emerging from th' intelligible deep,
Beauty's transcendent, solitary Sun.

THE EMPEROR JULIAN'S ORATION TO THE SOVEREIGN SUN

IT appears to me that the present oration very properly belongs to all--who breathe or creep on earth, who participate of being, of a rational soul, and of intellect; but I consider it as particularly belonging to myself; for I am an attendant of the sovereign Sun: and of the truth of this, indeed, I possess most accurate assurances, one of which it may be lawful for me, without envy, to relate. A vehement love for the splendors of this god took possession of me from my youth; in consequence of which, while I was a boy, my rational part was ravished with astonishment as often as I surveyed his etherial light; nor was I alone desirous of stedfastly beholding his diurnal splendors, but likewise at night, when the heavens were clear and serene, I was accustomed to walk abroad, and, neglecting every other concern, to gaze on the beauty of the celestial regions with rapturous delight: indeed I was so lost in attentive vision, that I was equally unconscious of another's discourse, and of my own conduct on such occasions. Hence I appeared to be too studious of their contemplation, and too curious in such employments; and, in consequence of this, though I was yet short of the perfection of manhood, I was suspected by some to be skilled in astronimical divination; but, indeed, no book of this kind was as yet in my possession, and I was entirely ignorant of its meaning and use. But why do I relate such trifling particulars, when I have things of far greater moment to declare, if I should tell my conceptions of the gods at that period of life. However, let the darkness of childhood be consigned to the shades of oblivion. But that the celestial light, with which I was every way environed, so excited and exalted me to its contemplation, that

I observed by myself the contrary course of the moon to that of the universe, before I met with any who philosophized on these subjects, may easily be credited from the indications which I have previously related. Indeed I admire the felicity of the man on whom divinity bestows a body united from sacred and prophetic seed, that he may disclose the treasuries of wisdom; but, at the same time, I will not despise the condition allotted me by the benefit of this deity; I mean, that I rank among those to whom the dominion and empire of the earth at the present period belong.

It is, indeed, my opinion, that the sun (if we may credit the wise) is the common father of all mankind; for as it is very properly said, man and the sun generate man. But this deity disseminates souls into the earth not from himself alone, but from other divinities; and these evince by their lives the end of their propagation. And his destiny will indeed be most illustrious, who, prior to his third progeny, and from a long series of ancestors, has been addicted to the service of this deity: nor is this to be despised, if some one, knowing himself to be naturally a servant of this god, alone among all, or with a few of mankind, delivers himself to the cultivation of his lord.

Let us then, to the best of our ability, celebrate his festival, which the royal city renders illustrious by its annual sacrifices and solemn rites. But I am well aware how difficult it is to conceive the nature of the unapparent sun, if we may conjecture from the excellence of the apparent god; and to declare this to others, can perhaps be accomplished by no one without derrogating from the dignity of the subject; for I am fully convinced that no one can attain to, the dignity of his nature: however, to possess a mediocrity in celebrating his majesty, appears to be the summit of human attainments. But may Mercury, the ruling deity of discourse, together with the Muses, and their leader, Apollo, be present in this undertaking; for this oration pertains to Apollo; and may they enable me so to speak of the immortal gods, that the credibility of my narration may be grateful and acceptable to their divinities. What mode of celebration then shall we adopt? Shall we, if we speak of his nature and origin, of his power and energies, as well manifest as occult, and besides this, of the communication of good which he largely distributes to every world, shall we, I say, by this means, frame an encomium, not perfectly abhorrent from the god? Let us therefore begin our oration from hence.

That divine and all-beautiful world, then, which, from the supreme arch of the heavens, to the extremity of the earth, is contained by the immutable providence of the deity, existed from eternity without any generation, and will be eternal through all the following periods of time; nor is it guarded by any other substance, than by the proximate investiture of the fifth body, the summit of which is the solar ray, situated, as it were, in the second degree from the intelligible world: but it is more antiently comprehended by the king and moderator of all things, about whom the universe subsists. This cause therefore, whether it is lawful to call him that which is superior to intellect; or the idea of the things which are, (but whom I should call the intelligible whole;) or the one, since the one appears to be the most antient of all things; or that which Plato is accustomed to denominate the good; this uniform cause, then, of the universe, who is to all beings the. administrator of beauty, perfection, union, and immeasurable power, according to a primary nature abiding in himself, produced from himself as a medium between the middle intellectual and demiurgic causes, that mighty divinity the sun perfectly similar to himself. And this was the opinion of the divine Plato, when he says: "This is what I called the son of the good, which the good generated analogous to itself: that as this in the intelligible place is to intellect and the objects of intelligence, so is that in the visible place to sight and the objects of sight." Hence it appears to me, that light has the same proportion to that which is visible, as truth to that which is intelligible, But this intelligible universe, as it, is the progeny of the idea of the first and greatest good, eternally abiding about his stable essence, obtains the supremacy among the intellectual gods; and is the, source of the same perfection to these, as the good to the intelligible gods. But according to my opinion, good is to intelligibles the cause of beauty, essence, perfection, and union; comprehending and illuminating their nature by its boniform power: the sun therefore distributes the same excellences to the intellectual gods, of whom he is appointed the sovereign ruler by the ordination of the good. At the same time, it must be observed, that these. gods are coexistent with this intellectual sun; by means of which, as it appears to me, from exerting a boniform cause among the intellectual gods, he administers all things according to the invariable rectitude of intellect.

But besides this, the third divine principle, I mean the apparent and splendid orbicular sun, is the cause of well-being to sensible natures; and whatever we have asserted as flowing from the mighty intellectual sun among the intellectual gods, the same perfections the apparent sun communicates to apparent forms; and the truth of this will be clearly evinced by contemplating invisible natures, from the objects of sensible inspection. Let us then begin the contemplation. And, in the first place, is not light the incorporeal and divine form of that which is diaphanous in energy? But whatever that which is diaphanous may be, which is subjected to all the elements, and is their proximate form, it is certain that it is neither corporeal nor mixt, nor does it display any of the peculiar qualities of body. Hence you cannot affirm that heat is one of its properties, nor its contrary cold; you can neither ascribe to it hardness nor softness, nor any other tangible difference; nor attribute taste or smell as peculiarities of its essence: for a nature of this kind, which is called forth into energy by the interposition of light, is alone subject to the power of sight. But light is the form of a diaphanous essence, which resembles that common matter, the subject of bodies, through which it is every where diffused; and rays are the summit, and as it were, flower of light, which is an incorporeal nature. But according to the opinion of the Phœnicians, who are skilled in divine science and wisdom, the universally-diffused splendor of light is the sincere energy of an intellect perfectly pure; and this doctrine will be found agreeable to reason, when we consider, that since light is incorporeal, its fountain cannot be body, but the sincere energy of intellect, illuminating in its proper habitation the middle region of the heavens: and from this exalted situation scattering its light, it fills all the celestial orbs with powerful vigor, and illuminates the universe with divine and incorruptible light.

But the operations of this pure intellect on the gods we have already briefly exhibited, and we shall shortly more largely discuss; for whatever we first perceive by the sight, is nothing but a mere name of honourable labour, unless it receives the ruling assistance of light: for how can any thing be visible unless, like matter, it is moved to the artificer that it may receive the supervening investments of form? Just as gold in a state of simple fusion is indeed gold, but is not a statue or an image till the artificer invests it with form: in a similar manner all naturally visible objects cease to be apparent unless light is present with the perceiver. Hence, since it confers vision on the perceiver, and visibility on the objects of perception, it perfects two natures in energy, sight and that which is visible; but perfections are form and essence; though perhaps an assertion of this kind is more subtle than is suited to our present purpose. However, of this all men are persuaded, both the scientific and the illiterate, philosophers and the learned, that day and night are fabricated by the power of this rising and setting divinity; and that he manifestly changes and convolves the world. But to which of the other stars does a province of this kind belong? Do we not therefore derive conviction from hence, that the unapparent and divine race of intellectual gods, above the heavens, are replenished from the sun with boniform powers; to whose authority the whole choir of the stars submits; and whose nod generation, which he governs by his providence, attentively obeys? For the planets, indeed, dancing round him as their king, harmoniously revolve in a circle, with definite intervals, about his orb; producing certain stable energies, and advancing backwards and forwards: (terms by which the skilful in the spheric theory signify such like phænomena of the stars) to which we may add, as manifest to every one, that the light of the moon is augmented or diminished according to her distance from the sun.

Is it not then highly probable, that the ordination of the intellectual gods, which is more antient than that of bodies, is analogous to the mundane disposition? Hence we infer his perfective power from the whole phænomena, because he gives vision to visive natures; for he perfects these by his light. But we collect his demiurgic and prolific power from the mutation of the universe; and his capacity of connecting all things into one, from the properties of motion conspiring into union and consent; and middle position, from his own central situation. Lastly, we infer his royal establishment among the intellectual gods, from his middle order between the planets; for if we perceived these, or as many other properties, belonging to any other of the apparent gods, we should not ascribe the principality among the gods to the sun. But if he has nothing in common with the rest, except that benificent power which he imparts to all, we ought to rely on the testimony of the Cyprian priests, who raised common altars to Jupiter and the Sun; or, indeed, prior to these, we should confide in Apollo, who is the attendant of this god; for thus he speaks: Jupiter, Pluto, Serapis, and the Sun, are one. And thus we should consider that there is a common, or rather one and the same principality, among the intellectual gods, of Jupiter and the Sun; hence as it appears to me, Plato does not absurdly call Pluto a prudent god; whom we also denominate Serapis, as if he were ἅιδῆσ, i.e. invisible and intellectual; to whom, according to his relation, the souls of those are elevated who have lived most wisely and just. For we must not conceive a Pluto of that kind, such as fables describe, horrid to the view; but one benevolent and mild, who perfectly liberates souls from the bands of generation, and fixes such as are not liberated in other bodies, that he may punish them for their guilt, and absolve the decisions of justice. Add too, that he likewise leads souls on high, and elevates them to the intelligible world.

But that this is not a recent opinion, but embraced by the most antient of poets, Homer and Hesiod, whether this arose the conceptions of their minds, or whether from a divine afflatus, as is usual with poets, enthusiastically energizing about truth, is evident from hence: for the one describing the genealogy of the sun, says, that he descended from Hyperion and Thea, that he may by this means evince, that he is the legitimate progeny of the super-eminent god; for how can we otherwise interpret the epithet Hyperion? And as to what pertains to the apellation Thea, is he not, after another mode, denominated by this means the most divine of beings? Nor must we conceive, with respect to his nature, that there is any copulation of bodies, or intervention of nuptials, which are the incredible and paradoxical sports of the poetic muse; but we must believe that his father and generator is most divine and supreme: and such will he be, who is above all things, about whom all things are placed, and for whose sake all things subsist. But Homer denominates him Hyperion from his father, that he may evince his perfect freedom and his superiority over all necessity: for Jupiter, who, as he says, is the lord of all, compels others to his will; but to this divinity, who threatened, on account of the impiety of Ulysses' companions, to forsake Olympus, he does not say,

"I heave the gods, the ocean, and the land;"

nor does he menace chains or the exertion of force; but promises vengeance on the authors of this impiety, and entreats him to continue to illuminate the gods. What else then can he mean to insinuate by this narration, but that this deity, exclusive of his perfect freedom, is of a telesiurgic nature, or is endued with a perfective operative power? For why would the gods require his assistance, unless by occultly illuminating their essence and being, he obtained a power of accomplishing the goods we have previously described? For when Homer says,

Meantime, unweary'd with his heav'nly way,
In ocean's waves th' unwilling light of day
Quench'd his red orb, at Juno's high command,

he indicates nothing more than that a premature opinion of night arose, through the intervention of horrid darkness: for of this goddess the poet thus speaks in another place:

Illustrious Juno then before them spread
A mist profound.---------------------------

But we shall take our leave of the poets, because they mingle much of human imperfection with the excellence of divinity; however, what this deity appears to have taught concerning himself and others, we shall now endeavour to unfold.

The region surrounding this earth has its being entirely in generation, or in an ever flowing subsistence (ἐν τῳ γίνεσθαι).

Who is it then that confers perpetuity on its nature? Is it not he, who comprehends it in limited measures! For the nature of body cannot be infinite; since it is neither without generation nor self subsistent: but if any thing should be continually produced from an apparent existence, without being resolved into it again, the essence of things in generation would be no more. Hence the solar god, exciting a nature of this kind with a sure and measured motion, raises and invigorates it as he approaches, and diminishes and destroys it as he recedes; or rather he vivifies it by his progress, moving and pouring into generation the rivers of life. But when he deserts one hemisphere and is transferred into another, he brings destruction on corruptible natures. And, indeed, the communication of good, originating from this divinity, equally diffuses itself on the earth: for it is participated by different regions at different periods; so that generation will never fail, nor will the god confer his beneficence on the passive world with any variations of good: for as there is a sameness of essence, so likewise of energy among the gods; especially in the sun, the king of the universe, whose motion is the most simple of all the natures, revolving contrary to the course of the world. And it is by this argument that the illustrious Aristotle proves his superiority to the rest: but a power by no means obscure is imparted to the world from the other intellectual gods. What then? Are we to exclude these while we confer sovereignty on the sun? By no means; for we endeavour to procure credibility, concerning unapparent essences, from such as are manifest and known. Hence, as he gives perfection, and harmonizes both to himself and to the universe, the power proceeding from the rest, and diffused on the earth, so it is proper to believe, that in the secret recesses of their natures they have a conjunction with each other; the sun, indeed, possessing the principality, while the rest conspire into union and consent with his divinity.

But as we have asserted that he is allotted a middle situation between the middle intellectual gods, what this middle station may be, in the midst of which he is established, may the sovereign sun enable me to explain. By a medium, therefore, in this place, we mean not that which is observed in contraries, and is equally distant from the extremes; as among colours, yellow, between white and black; or warmth, between heat and cold, and others of a similar nature; but that which unifies and copulates things divided and separate; such as is the harmony of Empedocles, from which he perfectly excluded strife and contention. What then are the natures which he connects, and of which he is said to be the medium? We reply, that he is the unifying medium of the apparent and mundane deities, and of the immaterial and intelligible gods, who surround the good; as he is an intelligible and divine essence multiplied without passivity, and augmented without addition. After this manner, then, the intellectual and all-beautiful essence of the royal sun, consists from no temperament of the extremes, but is perfect and free from all mixture, both of apparent and invisible, of sensible and intelligible gods. And thus we have declared the medium which it is proper to ascribe to his nature.

But if it be requisite to be more explicit, and to explain the medium of his essence, and how we may separately, and by species, understand his proportion to the first and last, though it is difficult to accomplish the whole of this arduous undertaking, yet we will attempt the explanation to the best of our ability. There is, then, an intelligible one perpetually pre-existent, who comprehends the universality of things in one. But what? Is not the whole world one animal, profoundly replenished with soul and intellect, and perfect from the conjunction of perfect parts? Hence, between this twofold unifying perfection, I mean that which in the intelligible place comprehends all things in one, and the other which is conversant about the world, and coalesces in one and the same perfect nature, the unifying perfection of the royal sun intervenes, seated in the midst of the intellectual gods. But, posterior to this, there is a certain connection of the gods in the intelligible world, harmonizing all things into one; for do not the heavens appear to revolve about the substance of the fifth body, which connects all their parts, and binds and establishes in itself their mutually dissoluble and flowing natures? Hence the royal sun so collects into one these two connecting essences, one of which is perceived in intelligibles, but the other in sensibles, that he perfectly imitates the connecting power in intellectuals, of which he is the source. But he presides and rules over that last unifying nature which is perceived about this apparent world. And I know not whether that which is called self-subsistent, which is first among intelligibles, but last in the celestial phænomena, possesses the middle, self-subsistent essence of the royal sun; from which first-operative' substance that splendor emanates which illumines every thing in the apparent world.

Again, that we may consider this affair in a different mode, since there is one demiurgus of the universe, but many demiurgic gods, who revolve round the heavens, it is proper to place in the midst of these the mundane administration of the sun: besides, the fertile power of life is copious and redundant in intelligibles, and the world is full of the same prolific life. Hence it is evident that the fertile life of the sovereign sun is a medium between the two, as the mundane phænomena perpetually evince. For, with respect to forms, some he perfects, and others he fabricates; some he adorns, and others he excites; nor is any thing capable of advancing into light and generation without the demiurgic power of the sun. Besides this, if we attend to the sincere, pure, and immaterial essence of intelligibles, to which nothing extrinsical flows, and nothing foreign adheres, but which is full of its own domestic simplicity, and afterwards consider the defecated nature of that pure and divine body which is conversant with mundane bodies revolving in an orb, and which is free from all elementary mixture, we shall find that the splendid and incorruptible essence of the royal sun, is a medium between the immaterial purity of intelligibles and that which in sensibles is sincere and remote from generation and corruption. But the greatest argument for the truth of this is derived from hence, that the light which flows from the sun upon the earth will not suffer itself to be mingled with any thing; nor is it polluted by any sordid nature, or by any contagion; but it abides every where pure, undefiled, and impassive. Again, if we consider not only immaterial, and intelligible forms, but such as are sensible, subsisting in matter, the middle intellectual situation of forms about the mighty sun will be no less certain and clear: for these afford continual assistance to forms merged in matter; so that they could neither exist, nor preserve themselves in existence, unless this beneficent deity co-operated with their essence. In short, is he not the cause of the secretion of forms and the concretion of matter? from whom we not only possess the power of understanding his nature, but from whom our eyes are endued with the faculty of sight? for the distribution of rays throughout the world, and union of light, exhibit the demiurgic secretion of the artificer.

But as there are many apparent goods in the essence of this divinity which demonstrate his middle position between the intelligible and mundane gods, let us pass on to the last and apparent condition of the sun. His first condition then about the last world is, that of the solar angels, whose idea and hypostasis is situated in their paradigm or exemplar. But, posterior to this, his power generative of sensibles succeeds; whose more honourable part contains the cause of the heavens and the stars, and whose inferior part presides over generation, at the same time comprehending eternally in itself an essence invariably the same. But indeed no one can explain all that is contained in the essence of this god, though intelligence should be conferred on him by this divinity himself; since intellect appears to me incapable of comprehending the whole.

It will here however be proper to set a seal, as it were, to our much-extended oration, that we may pass on to other disquisitions, which require a contemplation by no means inferior to the former: but what this seal may be, and what the conception of his essence, who summarily comprehends the universality of things, may the god himself inform my understanding; as I am desirous of comprehending with brevity from what principle he proceeds, in what his nature consists, and with what goods he replenishes the apparent world. We must assert, therefore, that from one god, I mean from one intelligible world, one sovereign sun proceeds, constituted in the middle of the intellectual gods, according to an all-various mediocrity; who connecting concordant and friendly natures, and such as, though distant, conspire into friendship and consent, conciliates in unity first natures with the last; containing in himself the middle of perfection, and connection of prolific life and uniform essence: who, besides this, is the author of every good to the sensible world, not only illuminating and adorning it by his splendour, but giving the same subsistence with himself to the essence of solar angels, and comprehending an unbegotten cause of generated natures; and, prior to this, containing a cause of eternal bodies free from the depredations of age, and endued with stability of life.

And thus far our oration has extended concerning the essence of the god; in which, though we have omitted many things, we have delivered not a few. But because the copiousness of his powers, and the beauty of his energies, are so great, that the properties considered in his essence vehemently excel: (for such is the condition of divine natures, that when they proceed into apparent form, they are multiplied through a redundancy and fecundity of life,) consider what occasion there is, that we who are as yet scarcely refreshed from the preceding long oration, should venture on an immense ocean of enquiry. Let us, however, dare the investigation, trusting in the assistance of the god, and endeavour to accomplish our discourse.

In the first place, then, we must consider that whatever we have previously asserted concerning his essence, belongs in common to his powers; for the essence of the god is not one thing, his power another, and his energy a third; since all that he wishes, he both is, and can be, and produces in energy: for neither does he wish to be that which he is not, nor is he unable to become what he wishes, nor does he wish to energize what he cannot effect. The case indeed is very different with respect to mankind; for in man a twofold and discordant nature is discerned conciliated into one, i.e. the nature of soul and body; the former of which is divine, and the latter shadowy and dark, the source of contention and strife. Hence, as Aristotle observes, neither pleasures nor griefs are in amicable conjunction with our nature; for what is pleasant to the one procures molestation to its contrary, the other. But among the gods nothing of this kind subsists; for their essence supplies them with good, invariably, and in a perpetual series. Whatever therefore we have asserted for the purpose of explaining his essence, the same must be applied to his powers and energies. But since our oration appears to reciprocate in these, it follows that we must consider in our subsequent speculations about his powers and energies, that these are not his operations only, but his essence: for there are certain divinities allied to, and connate with, the sun, who augment the pure essence of the god, and who, though they are multiplied in the world, yet subsist uniformly about the sun.

But attend, in the first place, to their assertions who have not contemplated the heavens, like horses, or oxen, or other irrational and brutal animals, but have laboured to investigate an unapparent nature from sensible appearances. And prior to this, you may, if so inclined, speculate a little concerning his supermundane powers and energies. Of these powers, the first is that by which he causes the whole of an intellectual essence to appear profoundly one, by collecting extremes into one and the same; for as we clearly perceive in the sensible world that air and water are situated between fire and earth, for the purpose of connecting the extremes as by a bond, there is no reason why we should not admit a similar establishment in an essence prior to body and separate from its nature; which obtains the principle of generation, and is itself superior to origin. Hence, in an essence of this kind, as well as among elementary forms, the extreme principles which are separated from all corporeal commerce being through certain mediums collected into one by the royal sun, become united about his nature: and with this indeed the demiurgic power of Jupiter accords; to whom, as we have previously related, temples were dedicated in Cyprus in common with the sun. In the same place, too, we have brought the testimony of Apollo in confirmation of its truth, who doubtless understands his nature better than the wisest of mankind; for he is present and communicates with the sun, possessing the same simplicity of intellection, stability of essence, and sameness of energy. For Apollo appears by no means to separate from the sun the multiplied and partial operation of Bacchus, but rather, as he perpetually subjects him to the sun, and demonstrates him to be his attendant, he assists us in framing the most beautiful conceptions about the god. Besides, so far as the sun contains in himself the principles of the most beautiful intellectual temperament, he becomes Apollo, the leader of the Muses; but so far as he accomplishes the elegant order of the whole of life, he generates Esculapius in the world; whom at the same time he comprehended in himself prior to the world.

But though we may contemplate many powers of the god, yet we can never exhaust the whole. This, however, ought to suffice us, that in a nature separate from, and more antient than, body, and in a genus of causes abstracted from appearances, we may contemplate an equal, and the same principallity and power of Jupiter and the sun. We may likewise survey a simplicity of intelligence, together with perpetuity, and a stability of sameness, united with Apollo; but divisibility of operation, in conjunction with Bacchus, who presides over a partial essence. Add to, that we may perceive the power of beautiful symmetry and intellectual temperament in union with Musagetes. And lastly, we may conceive that power which fills up the elegant order of the whole of life as combined with Esculapius. And thus much concerning the supermundane powers of the god; whose correspondent operations above the apparent world consist in diffussing a perpetual plenitude of good; for as he is the genuine progeny of the good, from whom he receives a perfect and beneficent condition, he distributes this excellency of his nature to all the intellectual gods, assigning them an essence benignant and perfect. But another employment of the god consists in conferring an absolute distribution of intelligible beauty among intellectual and incorporeal forms; for as the generative essence apparent in nature desires to beget in the beautiful and to expose its progeny to the light, it is necessary that an essence should antecede and be the leader of this, which eternally generates in intelligible beauty: at the same time we must observe that it does not operate at one time and not at another; or beget at one period and become afterwards barren; for whatever is sometimes beautiful here, is perpetually fair among intelligible natures. Hence we must assert, that an unbegotten progeny, subsisting in intellectual and eternal beauty, antecedes every prolific cause in the apparent world: and this progeny the sun contains, and establishes about his own essence; conferring on him a perfect intellect, and by this means giving sight, as it were, to his eyes by the benefit of his light. In a similar manner, in the intelligible world, by means of an intellectual paradigm, which scatters a light far brighter than ethereal splendor, he extends, as it appears to me, the power of intellection, and of being intelligible, to all intellectual natures. But, besides this, there is another admirable energy belonging to the sun, the king of the universe; I mean that better condition which he attributes to the more excellent genera of beings, such as angels, dæmons, heroes, and partial souls, who perpetually abide in the reason of their exemplar and idea without merging themselves in the darkness of body. And thus we have hastily explained, to the best of our ability, the supermundane essence of the god, by celebrating its powers and operations in that universal king the sun. But since the eyes (as it is said) are more worthy of belief than the ears, though they deserve less credibility, and are more imbecil than intelligence, let us now consider his apparent fabrication, having first intreated his pardon, for endeavouring, with moderate abilities, to celebrate his divinity.

The apparent world then, perpetually subsists about the sun; and his light, which surrounds the universe, obtains an eternal seat; so as not to be subject to any variations of place, since it is for ever the same. But if any one is willing to conceive by mere thought alone this eternal nature as temporal, he will easily know respecting the sun, the king of the universe, who immediately illuminates every thing with his light, what abundant goods he eternally confers on the world. I am not indeed ignorant that both the great Plato, and Jamblichus of Chalcis, who was posterior to Plato in time, though not in the powers of mind, and to whose books I am indebted for other philosophical information, as well as the present arcana, consider the sun as generated for hypothesis only; and establish a certain temporal production for the sake of disputation, that we may be able to comprehend the magnitude of his effects. But this is on no account to be attempted by me, who am inferior to them in all mental endowments; especially since the very hypothesis of his temporary production is not without danger, as was evident to that illustrious hero Jamblichus himself. However, since this god proceeded from an eternal cause, or rather produced all things from eternity, generating such as are apparent at present from unapparent causes, by a divine will, an ineffable celerity, and an invincible power: hence he is allotted the middle region of the heavens, as more accommodated to his nature, that he may afford to the gods, produced from, and together with him, an equal distribution of good; and besides this, that he may preside over the eight spheres of the heavens; and may govern the ninth fabrication, which possesses an eternal vicissitude in generation and decay. For as to the planets, it is manifest, that, dancing, as it were, round the sun, their motions are measured by a certain symphony of figures with respect to the god; to which we may add, that the whole heavens harmonizing with him in all their parts, are replenished with gods from his divinity: for this god presides over the five celestial orbs, and by revolving round three of these, generates as many Graces, while the rest are called the balances of mighty Necessity. But these observations are perhaps more obscure to the Greeks, and on that account unacceptable; as if we should relate nothing but what is common and known.

But indeed they are by no means unusual and strange; for who (O ye most wise, and without inquiry assenting to a multitude of assertions) are the Dioscuri? Are they not said to live on alternate days, because it is not lawful for both of them to be apparent on the same day; as, for instance, that you may clearly understand me, yesterday and today? Then again, consider with respect to the same Dioscuri, endeavouring with me to adapt your conceptions to their nature, lest we should assert any thing new and unintelligible. But indeed we shall find nothing of this kind, though we scrutinize in the most accurate manner: for the assertion of some theologists that they are the two hemispheres of the world, by no means pertains to the present investigation; since it is not easy to conceive why each of these is called ετερημερος, or diurnally alternate, as their illustration is gradually augmented without any sensation of diurnal increment.

But we are now entering upon speculations, in the course of which we may possibly appear to make some innovations. In the first place then, those may be very properly said to participate the same day, to whom an equal time of the solar progression, in one and the same month, belongs. Let any one now consider how this diurnal alternation can be accommodated, as well with other, as the tropical circles. But a speculation of this kind is not indeed adapted to our present investigation; because these circles are always apparent, and are conspicuous to the inhabitants of regions situated in opposite shadows, each to each; yet he who perceives the one cannot by any means discover the other. However, that we may not dwell any longer in explaining the present affair, the sun, as we know by his annual revolutions, is the parent of the seasons; and considered as never receding from the poles, he is the Ocean, the ruler of a two-fold essence; nor is such an assertion by any means obscure, since Homer, so long before us, calls Ocean the generation of mortals, of the blessed divinities, and of all things: and this indeed with the greatest truth and propriety; for there is nothing in the universe which is not the natural progeny of the Ocean. But are you willing I should explain in what respect this concerns the vulgar? Though perhaps it might be better to be silent, I will speak on this occasion: I will speak, though my discourse will not be properly received by all.

The solar orb, then, is moved in the starless, which is far higher then the inerratic sphere. Hence, he is not the middle of the planets, but of the three worlds, according to the mystic hypotheses; if it be proper to call them hypotheses, and not rather dogmata; confining the appellation of hypothesis to the doctrine of the sphere: for the truth of the former is testified by men who audibly received this information from gods, or mighty dæmons; but the latter is founded on the probability arising from the agreement of the phænomena. Hence, if any one should esteem it better both to praise and confide in the former, such a one, whether I am trifling or in earnest, will meet with my esteem and admiration.

But besides those which I have mentioned, there is an innumerable multitude of celestial gods, perceived by such as do not contemplate the heavens indolently and after the manner of brutes. As the sun quadruply divides these three worlds, on account of the communion of the zodiac with each, so he again divides the zodiac into twelve powers of gods, and each of these into three others, so that thirty-six are produced in the whole. Hence, as it appears to me, a triple benefit of the Graces proceeds to us from the heavens, I mean from those circles which the god quadruply dividing produces in consequence of this, a quadripartite beauty and elegance of seasons and times. But the Graces also imitate a circle in their resemblances on the earth. Add too, that Bacchus is the source of joy, who is said to obtain a common kingdom with the sun. But why should I here mention the epithet Horus, or other names of the gods, all of which correspond with the divinity of the sun? Mankind, indeed, may conceive the excellence of the god from his operations; since he perfects the heavens with intellectual goods, and renders them partakers of intelligible beauty. For as he originates from this beauty, he applies himself, both totally and by parts, to the distribution of good . . . . These gods indeed preside over all motion, as far as to the utmost boundaries of the world; so that both nature and soul, and every thing that exists, is perfected by their beneficent communications. But the sun combining this abundant army of gods into one ruling unity, confers on it the providence of Minerva; who originated, according to fables, from the head of Jupiter; but who, according to our opinion, proceeded from the whole of the sovereign sun, and is wholly comprehended in his nature. Hence we differ from fables in this, that we do not consider her as springing from the summit, but as totally born from the whole of Jupiter; for by conceiving no difference between Jupiter and the sun, we shall think agreeable to the decisions of the antients. And, indeed, by calling the sun providential Minerva, we shall not assert any thing new, if we properly understand the following verse. "he came to Python, and to providential Minerva." For thus the antients seated Minerva with Apollo, who appears to differ in nothing from the sun. And I know not whether Homer, by a certain divine instinct, (for it is probable that he was seized with a divine fury,) prophesies this, when he sings,

So might my life, and glory know no bound,
Like Pallas worship'd, like the Sun renown'd.

That is to say, like Jupiter, who is the same with the sun. And as the king Apollo, on account of his simplicity of intellection, communicates with the sun, so likewise it is proper to believe that Minerva, since she receives her essence from this deity, and is his perfect intellection, combines into union, without any confusion, the gods who surround the sovereign sun; and that the same goddess, from the summit of heaven, pours through the seven planetary orbs, as far as to the moon, the genuine and pure rivers of life; indeed she fills the moon, who is the last of the orbicular bodies, with intelligence; and thus causes her to contemplate the intelligibles above the heavens, to regard inferior natures, and to beautify matter with the investiture of forms, by removing from its shadowry essence whatever it contains, wild, turbulent, and destitute of order.

But the goods which Minerva confers on mankind are wisdom, intelligence, and operative arts: she is also said to obtain the towers of cities, because she establishes civil community by her wisdom. It is likewise proper to declare a few particulars respecting Venus, who, according to the learned among the Phœnicians, (which is likewise my opinion) has a demiurgic community with Minerva. Venus, then, is the temperament of the celestial gods, and the friendship and union, by which their harmony subsists; for as she is proximate to the sun, in conjunction with whom she revolves, she fills the heavens with the best temperament, gives fertility to the earth, and is the source of perpetuity to the generation of animals. And of all this the sovereign sun is the primary cause: but Venus concurs in her operations with this divinity; alluring our souls with pleasure, and diffusing from æther, delightful and incorruptible splendors on the earth, far superior to the brightest refulgence of gold. I am likewise desirous of disclosing a few arcana from the Phœnician theology; whether or not in vain, our oration will gradually disclose. Those, then, who inhabit Edessa, a region eternally dedicated to the sun, consider Monimus, and Azizus, as the attendants of this deity; Monimus, according to Jamblichus, (from whom we have received a few observations out of many,) being the same with Mercury and Azizus, the same as Mars; and each of them, in conjunction with the sun, diffusing a variety of goods on the earth.

Such, then, are the effects of this god in the heavens, and through these his perfections are propagated to the utmost boundaries of the earth: but as it would be arduous to enumerate all his operations beneath the moon, let us celebrate them by a compendious recital. I know, indeed, that I have already mentioned these, when I investigated the invisible properties of the god from the phænomena; but the order of my discourse requires that I should now resume the narration.

As therefore we have asserted that the sun obtains the principallity among the intellectual gods, whose impartible essence is surrounded with a great and uniform multitude of gods, as likewise that he is the leader and lord of the natures, which among sensibles revolve in an orb, with an eternal and blessed progression; and that as he fills the heavens with apparent splendor, so likewise with an infinite abundance of unapparent goods; from whose occult and divine energy too the goods derived from the other apparent gods receive their perfection; so likewise we must consider; that certain gods reside in the receptacle of generation, who are comprehended by the sovereign sun, and who governing the quadruple nature, are established about the souls of the elements, together with the three genera, more excellent than man. But consider what mighty goods he confers on partial souls! For to these he extends judgement, governs them by justice, and purifies them by his splendor. Besides this, does he not move and suscitate all nature, by imparting to it fecundity from on high? For he is the true cause of particular natures arriving at the destined end of their existence; since (as Aristotle observes) man and the sun generate man. Hence, we should form the same judgement, of the sovereign sun, in every other effect of particular natures: for does not the god fabricate for us rains and winds, and whatever else is produced in the aerial regions? Since, by giving heat to the earth he excites vapour and fume, by means of which, not only these sublime phænomena, but likewise subterranean events of greater or less importance, are produced.

But why should we protract this enumeration any farther, since it is now proper to hasten to the conclusion; first of all celebrating the goods which the sun bestows on mankind? For as he is the source of our existence, so likewise of the aliment by which that existence is supported. And indeed he confers on us more divine advantages peculiar to souls; for he loosens these from the bands of a corporeal nature, reduces them to the kindred essence of divinity, and assigns them the subtile and firm texture of divine splendor, as a vehicle in which they may safely descend to the realms of generation. And these benefits of the god have been celebrated by others according to their desert, and require the assent of faith more than the evidence of demonstration.

But we ought not to fear attempting the relation of such things as are naturally the objects of knowledge to all men. Plato, then, asserts that the heavens are the masters of wisdom to mankind, since it is from these that we learn the nature of number; and our knowledge of its diversity is solely derived from the revolution of the sun. To which Plato also adds, that the heavens, by the succession of many days and nights, never cease to instruct the dullest apprehensions in the art of numbering; and that this is also effected by the varying light of the moon, which is solely imparted to this goddess from the sun; indeed the farther we advance in our researches into wisdom of this kind, the more shall we every where perceive the symphony and consent of other deities with the sun. And this Plato himself evinces when he says, that the gods pitying the human race, which is naturally laborious and afflicted, gave to us Bacchus and the Muses, who perpetually combine in one harmonious choir. But the sun appears to be the common ruler of these, since he is celebrated as the father of Bacchus, and the leader of the Muses; for does not Apollo, whose government is united in amicable conjunction with these divinities, diffuse his oracles over all the earth? Does he not extend divinely-inspired wisdom to mankind, and adorn cities with sacred and political institutions? It is this divinity who, through the colonies of the Greeks, has civilized the greatest part of the globe, and disposed it to receive with less refluctance the authority of the Romans; who indeed are not only descended from a Grecian origin, but have adopted, and perpetually preserved, from the beginning to the end, the sacred rites of the Greeks, and their piety towards the gods. To which we may add, that the Romans have established a form of government by no means inferior to that of any of the cities which have enjoyed the best constitutions, but rather one excelling all the modes of political administration which have ever been adopted. And through these considerations, I consider the city of Rome as Grecian, both on account of its origin, and political institutions. But why, besides this, should I assert to you, how the sun, by generating Esculapius, has provided for the health and safety of all things? And how he imparts all-various virtue, while he sends to mankind Venus and Minerva in amicable conjunction? Like a provident guardian appointing, by immutable law, that the mixt nature of bodies should pursue no other end than the generation of its like. Hence, by the constant revolutions of this deity, all vegetable and animal tribes are excited to the propagation of natures similar to their own. Why again is it necessary, to celebrate the rays and light of the sun? For who does not perceive the dreadful aspect of the night, which is not illustrated either by the splendor of the moon or stars? So that from this circumstance alone, we may conjecture how great a good we obtain through the light derived from this resplendent god. But this light indeed he imparts perpetually, and without being interrupted by the intervening shades of night, to places where it is necessary, or the regions above the moon; but to us he benignantly affords a cessation from labour, through the friendly interposition of the night. Indeed there would be no bound to our oration if we should pursue every particular of this kind, since there is no good belonging to our existence which we do not receive as the gift of this divinity; whether it is perfectly imparted from him alone, or receives its consummation from him, through the ministry of other gods.

But this deity presides over the city of Rome, and on this account Jupiter, the celebrated father of all things, not only resides in its tower, together with Minerva, and Venus, but Apollo also resides on the Palatine hill, together with the sun himself, who is universally known to be the same with Apollo. But I will mention a few things out of a many, principally pertaining to the sun, and to us who are the descendants of Romulus, and Æneas. For Æneas, according to tradition, descended from Venus, who assists the operations of the sun, and is allied to his nature: and the son of Mars is reported to have been the founder of our city; which, however paradoxical and incredible, was abundantly confirmed by succeeding prodigies. However, as I am well aware, and have already mentioned, that Mars, who is called by the Edessenian Syrians, Azizus, is the forerunner of the sun, I shall not insist on this particular at present. But it may be asked, why is a wolf consecrated to Mars rather than to the sun? For they denominate from hence the space of a year Lycabas. Nor is this appellation assumed by Homer only, and the more illustrious Greeks, but by a god himself; for thus he speaks: "Accomplishing, by a leaping progression, Lycabas, the path of twelve months."

Are you willing therefore that I should demonstrate by a more powerful argument, that the founder of our city not only descended from Mars, but that however the martial, and noble dæmon, who is said to have met with Silvia carrying the bath of the goddess, might contribute to the fabrication of his body, yet the soul of the god Quirinus wholly proceeded from the sun? For we ought, I think, to believe in general report. As therefore the conjunction of the sun and moon, who distribute in common the principallity of apparent natures, sent his soul on the earth, so likewise this conjunction received it back again from earth into the heavens, after it had consumed by the fire of thunder whatever was mortal in his corporeal frame. And from hence it is evident that the demiurgic goddess of terrene concerns, who is in a most perfect manner subjected to the sun, received our Quirinus, when he was sent by providential Minerva on the earth; and afterwards brought him back, when flying from. this terrene abode, to the sun, the sovereign of the world. But if you are desirous, besides this, that I should employ another argument on the same subject, derived from the works of King Numa, behold the unextinguished fire, enkindled from the sun which is preserved among us by sacred virgins according to the different seasons of the year; and which, by this means, imitates the beneficent energy of the moon in her revolution round the earth.

But I am able to produce another, and a much more indubitable argument, concerning this god, from the institutions of that most divine king. For while all other nations number their months from the course of the moon, we alone, together with the Egyptians, measure the days of our year from the revolutions of the sun. To all which, if I should add that we celebrate Mithras, and institute quadrennial contests in honour of the sun, I should speak of things more recent and known: but it will be better perhaps to adduce one testimony from more antient traditions.

Different nations then differently determine the commencement of the annual circuit; for some reckon from the vernal equinox; some from the middle of summer; most from autumn in its decline: yet all these celebrate the most apparent gifts of the sun. For some with grateful recollection honour the god for the opportunity afforded them in autumn for rustic labour; when the earth, pouring from her kindly womb all-various fruits, is cloathed with fertility, and every where exhibits the appearance of splendid hilarity; when the sea smooths its waters for the convenience of navigation; and the stormy brow of winter is changed into festive serenity.

But others derive the origin of their year from the summer day; because at that time they have greater security with respect to the success of fruits; since the various seeds deposited in the earth are at that period collected together; apples are in their most flourishing state; and the depending fruit of trees has acquired maturity through the benevolent heat of the solar fire. But others more elegant than these, establish the end of the year, when every fruit has acquired its most perfect vigor, and is tending to decay; and on this account, when autumn is in its decline, they date the commencement of their year. But our ancestors having learned from that most divine King Numa, to be more studious in venerating this divinity than other nations, without paying so much attention to what is useful, (acting in this respect in a manner becoming men of a divine nature and excellent understanding) directed their attention rather to the cause of these effects, and commanded the people to bind their heads at that period of the year, when the sun, having left the last meridian limit, returns to us again, and bending his course towards Capricorn, as to his destined goal, proceeds from the south to the north, that he may impart, by such a progression, his annual benefits to mankind. And from hence we may conjecture, that an attentive consideration of this particular induced our ancestors to establish this period as the beginning of the year; for they do not perform this annual ceremony on the day in which the sun commences his revolution, but when his progression from the meridian to the north is universally apparent: for as yet the subtility of those canons was not sufficiently known, which were discovered by the Chaldeans and Egyptians, and perfected by Hipparchus and Ptolomy. But forming their judgment solely from the testimony of the senses, they pursued the celestial phænomena: those of a more modern period, perceiving at the same time the rectitude of their observations. Hence, immediately on the close of the last month, which is dedicated to Saturn, and prior to the beginning of the new year, we celebrate most magnificent games in honour of the sun, whom we denominate unconquered; and, in conjunction with these games, it is unlawful to exhibit any of those sorrowful spectacles which necessarily pertain to the last month of the year.

But after the Saturnalia, which are the last of all, the Helian ceremonies return with the revolving year. And I sincerely wish that the sovereign gods would frequently permit me to celebrate and engage in these sacred festivals, and particularly that the sun, the king of the universe, would grant me permission, who from eternity is produced about the prolific essence of the good, as a harmonizing medium, between the middle intellectual gods; on whom he confers indissoluble connection, infinite beauty, affluent fecundity, perfect intellect, and an eternal accumulation of every good: who, in an indivisible moment, illuminates his conspicuous seat, which he eternally obtains in the middle region of the heavens: who imparts his intellectual beauty to this visible universe, and fills all the celestial regions with as many gods as he comprehends intellectually in himself, multiplied indivisibly about him, and uniformly conjoined with his essence. Nor does he less comprehend in his divinity the sublunary region, through a perpetuity of generation, and a communication of goods derived through a circular body; at the same time extending his providential care to the whole human race, and privately protecting the city of Rome. To which I may add, that he has generated my soul from eternity, and rendered it an attendant on his divinity. May he, therefore, communicate these gifts, and such others as we have already earnestly implored him to impart. But may he bestow on our city in common a perpetual duration, and benevolently preserve it from hostile devastation. And lastly, may he confer upon me, so long as he shall supply the streams of life, felicity and prosperity in whatever pertains to human and divine concerns: but may I live, and administer public affairs, as long as shall be pleasing to his divinity, useful to myself, and advantageous to the common affairs of the Romans.

And such, dear Sallust, is the oration, which, being mostly composed in the space of three nights, according to the triple administration of the god, and from the suggestions of memory at the time, I have dared to submit to your inspection; since a former piece of my composition on the Saturnalia, did not appear to you entirely foreign from the purpose, and undeserving your esteem. But if you are desirous of more perfect, and mystic discourses on this subject, by revolving the books of the divine Jamblichus, composed with the same design as the present oration, you will find the perfect consummation of human wisdom. But may the mighty sun, nevertheless, enable me to understand whatever pertains to his divinity; and to impart my information to all men in common, and privately to those who are worthy of such instruction. In the mean time, till the god shall crown my desires in this respect with success, let us both venerate Jamblichus, the friend of this divinity, from whom we have committed to writing a few particulars out of many which occurred to our recollection at the time: for I well know that no one can speak more perfectly on this subject than Jamblichus; though by the most vigorous contention, he should endeavour to add something of novelty to his discourse; for by such an attempt, as it is reasonable to suppose, he would deviate from true conceptions of the god.

Indeed if I had composed the present oration merely for the sake of instructing others, the labour of writing on such a theme after Jamblichus would perhaps have been in vain: but since I had no other intention than to render thanks to this divinity by a hymn, and considered my end accomplished in speaking of his essence to the utmost of my ability, I do not think that I have misspent my time by the present composition. For the admonition of Hesiod,

Perform, according to your utmost power,
Pure, sacred rites, to the immortal gods.

is not only to be understood as necessary in sacrifices, but likewise in the praises of the gods. In the third place, therefore, I earnestly entreat the sun, the king of the universe, that he will be propitious to me for my affection to his divinity; that he will impart to me a good life; more perfect wisdom; a divine intellect; and a gentle departure from the present state in a convenient time, that I may ascend to his divinity, and abide with him, if possible, in perpetual conjunction. But if this be a reward too great for my conduct on this terrene abode, may I at least be united with him for many, and long-extended periods of time.

THE EMPEROR JULIAN'S ORATION TO THE MOTHER OF THE GODS

Is it therefore requisite that we should speak about particulars of this kind; and that we should divulge, by a written oration, things which it is not lawful to mention, and which are ineffable? I mean, who Attis or Gallus is; and who the mother of the gods: what the particulars are respecting her sacred rites; and on what account they were delivered to us at first: for they were delivered indeed by the most antient Phrygians, and were first of all received by the Greeks, not indeed indiscriminately, but by the Athenians, after they had learned by experience that they were very far from acting properly in deriding him who performed the orgies of the mother of the gods. For they report that Gallus was injuriously treated, and ejected by the Athenians as one who introduced novelties in divine concerns; and this because they did not as yet understand the properties of the goddess, and her agreement with Deo, Rhea, and Ceres. But this injurious conduct was followed by the avenging anger of the god, and an expiation of his wrath. For the priest of the Pythian god, who becomes the leader of the Greeks in all their illustrious undertakings, exhorted them to appease the anger of the mother of the gods; in consequence of which, as they report, a temple was raised to the goddess, in which all the public writings of the Athenians are preserved.

But after the Greeks, the Romans received the same sacred rites, the Pythian deity persuading them also to this undertaking, that they might procure the presence of the Phrygian goddess as a military associate in the Carthaginian war. And here perhaps it will not be improper to insert the following short history of this affair. As soon as the Romans had received the oracle of Apollo, the inhabitants of Rome, the friend of divinity, sent an ambassador to the kings of Pergamus, who then reigned in Phrygia, and ordered him to request of the Phrygians the most holy image of the goddess: but the ambassador receiving the sacred burthen, placed it in a good-sailing vessel, and which was in every respect well adapted to swim over such a length of sea. The ship therefore, having passed over the Ægean and Ionian, and sailed about the Sicilian and Tyrrhene sea, drove at length to the mouth of the Tyber. But then the common people of Rome, together with the senate, poured forth to the spectacle: and the priests and priestesses in particular were far more eager on this occasion than the rest; all of whom, invested with becoming ornaments, and such as were agreeable to the custom of their country, attentively fixed their eyes on the ship sailing with a prosperous course, and on the impetuosity of the parted billows as they dashed about the keel. But afterwards, when the ship drove into the port, each person adored the statue at a distance from the place where he happened to stand. But the goddess, as if willing to convince the Roman people that they had not led from Phrygia an inanimate image, but some thing endued with a greater and more divine power than ordinary [22], stopped the vessel as soon as it reached the Tyber, and suddenly rooted it, as it were, in the stream. Hence, on the people endeavouring to draw it against the tide, it resisted their efforts, and remained fixed; nor did it in the least yield to their attempts of thrusting it forward; and though every artifice was employed for this purpose, yet it still remained immovable. In consequence of this, a dire and unjust suspicion arose against the all-sacred priesthood of the consecrated virgin; and Clodia (for this was the name of the venerable virgin) was accused as one not perfectly pure, and who had not preserved herself inviolate to the goddess; and hence it was said, the divinity gave evident tokens of indignation and wrath; for it now appeared to every one that the image was something more divine than usual.

But in consequence of this suspicion, the virgin was at first filled with shame, so very remote was she from a conduct so unlawful and base. But when she perceived that the accusation against her gathered strength, then, unbinding her zone, and girding it round the extremity of the ship, like one agitated by divine inspiration, she ordered all the multitude to depart. Afterwards she entreated the goddess that she would not suffer her to be circumvented by unjust blasphemies: and then, as they report, raising her voice, as if she was giving a nautical signal, O, queen mother, (says she) if I am chaste, follow me. But after she had thus spoken, she not only moved the ship, but drew it for a considerable space along the stream. And these two circumstances the goddess exhibited to the Romans for the purpose, as it appears to me, of convincing them that they had not brought from Phrygia a burthen of inconsiderable honour, but one worthy the highest estimation, as not being any thing human but truly divine; nor a piece of inanimate earth, but an inspired and divine possession. This then was one of the particulars which the goddess exhibited to the Romans; but the other, that no citizen, whether virtuous or depraved, could be concealed from her inspection. And besides this, the Romans from that time warred on the Carthaginians with prosperous success.

These historical particulars therefore, though they may appear incredible to some, and neither adapted to a philosopher nor a theologist, ought, nevertheless, to be mentioned; for they are commonly related by most historians, and the representation of them is yet preserved in brazen images in Rome, the most powerful of cities, and beloved by the gods. Though I am not ignorant that some of the vehemently wise will consider these matters as the intolerable trifles of old women; but to me it appears more proper to give credit to cities in these affairs, than to such knowing men, whose little soul is indeed acute, but beholds nothing with a vision healthy and sound.

But I hear that Porphyry has philosophized about some of those particulars which I had an intention of discoursing upon during the time in which the sacred rites of the goddess were celebrated; but I know not what Porphyry has said on this occasion, nor have I yet met with his discourse on the subject, though it may happen that his opinion may be coincident with mine. But I (as the result of my own spontaneous conceptions on the occasion) understand by Gallus and Attis, the essence of that prolific and demiurgic intellect which generates all things even to the lowest matter, and which contains in itself all the reasons and causes of material forms: for the forms of all things do not subsist in all, nor are the ideas of the lowest and last of things, which possess nothing but the name of privation, with an obscure conception, in the most supreme and first of causes [23]. As therefore there are many essences, and many artificers of things, that nature of the third demiurgus, (who contains the exempt reasons, and continued causes, of material forms), which, descending from on high, through the stars, pervades through prolific abundance as far as to the earth, is that Attis who is the subject of our present investigation. But perhaps it is necessary to express my meaning more clearly.

We say then, that matter is something, and that there is also a material form; but unless we admit that there is a certain cause which has an establishment prior to these, we shall, through ignorance, verge to an Epicurean opinion: for if there be nothing more ancient than these two principles, the realms of generation must be alloted a rash and fortuitous impulse. But we may perceive (says a certain sagacious Peripatetic, such as Xenarchus) that the cause of these is a fifth and circular body [24]. But it appears to me that both Aristotle and Theophrastus are ridiculously anxious about a body of this kind, and that they are ignorant, as it were, of their own voice. For, as when we have arrived at an incorporeal and intelligible essence it is necessary to stop, and not to investigate any superior cause, but content ourselves with saying, that these things are thus naturally established, so, (say they) with respect to the fifth body, it is necessary to acknowledge that it naturally subsists in this manner; to explore no other causes, but to stop here, without ascending to an intelligible essence, which, as it is naturally in itself nothing, so it is nothing but an empty conception in the soul; for after this manner I remember to have heard Xenarchus discoursing; but whether he is right or not in such assertions, I shall leave to the first-rate Peripatetics to determine. That this, indeed, is not agreeable to my opinions on the subject, must be perfectly evident to every one; since I consider the hypotheses of Aristotle as wanting support, unless they are conciliated with those of Plato; or rather unless they are found to be consonant to the oracles of the gods.

But perhaps it is worth inquiring how a circular body is capable of containing the causes of material forms, for it is manifest and clear, that without these, generation cannot possibly subsist: for on what account are so many things generated? From whence do the male and female natures originate? From whence the difference of things subsisting according to genus in bounded forms, unless there are certain previously-subsisting and presiding reasons and causes which pre-exist as paradigms, and to the perception of which, if our sight is dull, we should still farther purify the eyes of our soul? But proper purgation consists in a conversion of the soul to itself, and a perception how soul and a material intellect are, as it were, certain express resemblances and images of immaterial [25] forms: for there is not any one body, or any thing incorporeal, which subsists and is beheld about bodies, the image of which intellect is not able to receive in an incorporeal manner; and this it could never be able to accomplish unless it possessed something naturally allied to these. On this account Aristotle also says, that the soul is the place of forms, not indeed in energy, but in capacity only [26]. It is necessary therefore that such a soul, and which converts itself to the body, should possess these in capacity: and if there is any soul unrestrained by, and unmixed with, the body, we ought to think that all things subsist in such a soul no longer in capacity but in perfect energy.

But we shall understand this more clearly by means of the paradigm which Plato employs in the Sophista, though for a purpose different from the present. But I do not introduce this example with a view to give demonstration to what has been said, for it is not proper to receive this by demonstration, but by a direct application of intellect [27] alone: for our discourse is about first principles, or things co-ordinate with such as are first; since Attis is considered by us, and with great propriety, as a god. But what, and of what kind, is this example? Plato then says, that, among those who are conversant with imitation, if any one wishes to imitate in such a manner as to emulate the real subsistence of the things imitated, such an undertaking will be laborious and difficult, and almost next to impossible; but that the imitation of things according to their appearance is easy, expeditious, and extremely possible. When, therefore, receiving a mirror, we carry it about, we may easily exhibit the representations of the several species of things. Let us now transfer the similitude of this example to the subject of our investigation; and let the mirror be that which is called by Aristotle the place in capacity of forms: but it is perfectly necessary that the forms themselves should subsist in energy prior to capacity. Since our soul therefore contains, as it appears to Aristotle, the forms of things in capacity, where shall we first place these as subsisting in energy? Shall we establish them in material natures? But these are evidently the last of things. It remains, therefore, that we should explore immaterial causes, which subsist in energy prior to material natures, and from which, having a prior subsistence, our soul necessarily receives the reasons of forms, in the same manner as a mirror the images of things. But from hence she imparts them through nature to matter, and to these material bodies: for we are certain that Nature [28] is the artificer of bodies, as a whole of the universe; but as subsisting in individuals, of every thing which has the relation of a part. But nature in energy subsists in us without phantasy; and soul above this is endued with phantasy. If therefore it be confessed that nature contains the cause of things of which she possesses no phantasy, what by the gods should hinder us from assigning this prerogative to soul, by a much better and more ancient right; since we know this very particular in a phantastic manner, and at the same time apprehend it by a reasoning energy? Besides, where is the person so contentious, who will allow that material reasons subsist in nature, all indeed in capacity, though not all according to the same in energy, and yet will not allow this to soul? If, therefore, forms subsist in nature in capacity, and not in energy [29], and likewise subsist in soul, but more pure and distinct, so as that they can be apprehended and known, but yet are by no means in energy; from whence do we derive the firm persuasion of the perpetuity of generation? Or where can our intellect find any stability in arguments respecting the eternity of the world? For a circular body is a composite of subject and form. It is necessary therefore, that though these are not separate from each other in energy, yet in our conceptions we should consider forms as having a prior and more ancient subsistence.

Since therefore it is admitted, that a certain preceding cause of material forms, in itself perfectly immaterial, is in subjection to the third artificer of things, who is not only the father and lord of these, but also of the apparent and fifth body; hence, separating Attis from this deity, as a cause descending as far as to matter, we are persuaded that Attis or Gallus is a prolific god. But, according to the fable, this god being placed near the whirling streams of the river Gallus, obtained a flourishing condition of being, and afterwards appearing beautiful and grand, was beloved by the mother of the gods; who, after she had committed all things to his charge, placed on his head a starry hat. But since this apparent heaven thus covers the head of Attis, is it proper to interpret the river Gallus as signifying the Gallaxy? For here a passive body is said to be mingled with the impassive circulation of the fifth body. And thus far the mother of the gods permitted this beautiful and intellectual god Attis, who is similar to the solar rays, to leap and dance. But when, in the course of his progression, he arrived at the extremity of things, the fable relates that he came into a cavern, and had connection with a nymph, obscurely signifying by this, the humid nature of matter [30]; though indeed matter is not so much signified here, as that last incorporeal cause which presides over matter; for, according to Heraclitus,

"Death is the portion of the humid soul."

Such, then, is the intellectual god Gallus, i.e. a deity who contains in himself material and sublunary forms, and who associates with the cause presiding over the fluctuating nature of matter. But he does not associate with the nymph as one with another of the same dignity and rank, but after the manner of one falling into matter. Who then is the mother of the gods? She is indeed the fountain of the intellectual and demiurgic gods who govern the apparent series of things: or certainly a deity producing things, and at the same time subsisting with the mighty Jupiter; a goddess mighty, after one mighty, and conjoined with the mighty demiurgus of the world. She is the mistress of all life, and the cause of all generation, who most easily confers perfection on her productions, and generates and fabricates things without passion, in conjunction with the father of the universe. She is also a virgin, without a mother, the assessor of Jupiter, and the true parent of all the gods: for receiving in herself the causes of all the intelligible supermundane gods, she becomes a fountain to the intellectual gods. The mother of the gods therefore, subsisting after this manner, and who is also called Providence, was inflamed with an impassive love of Attis: for she voluntarily comprehends not only material forms, but much more the causes of these. But, according to the fable, this divine providence, which preserves all generated and perishable natures, fell in love with their demiurgic and prolific cause, and exhorted him to generate rather in an intelligible nature, and to be willing to convert himself to her essence, and to dwell with her divinity; and lastly, she commanded him to associate with no other than herself.

But her intention in these injunctions was, that he might at the same time pursue a salutary union, and avoid verging to matter. Hence she ordered him to behold her, as she was the fountain of the demiurgic gods, and this without being drawn downwards or allured into generation. For by this means the mighty Attis would become an artificer in a more excellent degree; since in all things conversion to a better nature is more efficacious than a propensity to a worse condition of being. For the fifth body, indeed, is on this account more fabricative and divine than terrestrial natures, because it is more converted to the gods. But no one will dare to affirm that a body, though it should be composed of the purest æther, is better than an undefiled soul, such as the demiurgus assigned to Hercules: for his soul, prior to her incarnation, then was, and appeared to be, more efficacious than when she consented to a conjunction with body. For a providential attention to these inferior concerns is much easier to Hercules now, having wholly departed to his universal father [31], than it was formerly, when, being invested with flesh, he was educated among men. So much more efficacious to every nature is a conversion to that which is better, than an apostization to that which is worse. But the fable, desirous to signify this, says, that the mother of the gods exhorted Attis to take care of himself, and neither depart any where else, nor be captivated with any other. but Attis, departing from the mother of the gods, descended even to the very extremity of matter. Hence, since it was necessary that infinity should, some time or other, be restrained and stop in its progression, Corybas, or the mighty sun, who has the same establishment as the mother of the gods, who fabricated, and providentially governs, all things in conjunction with her, and who performs nothing without her, persuaded the lion to announce the descent of Attis into the lowest matter. Who then is the lion? We are told for a certainty that he was yellow: he is therefore a cause presiding over a hot and fiery nature; which cause was hereafter to contend with a nymph and emulate her association with Attis.

But who the nymph is, we have already explained: and the lion is said to be subservient to the demiurgic providence of things, i.e. without doubt, to the mother of the gods; and afterwards by his detecting and betraying Attis, to have been the cause of his castration. But castration [32] is a certain repression of infinity: for things in generation are not established in bounded forms, and restrained by a demiurgic providence, without that which is called the insanity of Attis; which, when it departs from measure, and transcends all bound, becomes, as it were, debilitated, and is no longer able to preserve the prerogative of its nature. And it is not irrational to believe that this should take place about the last cause among the gods. Behold, therefore, the fifth body unaltered according to every variation, and terminated by the illuminations of the moon, that this rising and perishing world may be in the vicinity of the fifth body. For, in the illuminations of the moon, we perceive that a certain variation and passion takes place. It is by no means therefore absurd to assert, that Attis is a certain demigod, (for this is the meaning of the fable) or rather he is in reality a god: for he proceeds from the third demiurgus, and after his castration is again recalled to the mother of the gods; but as he persuaded himself wholly to verge, he appears to incline [33] into matter. Indeed he who considers this deity as the last of the gods, but the head of all the divine genera, will by no means deviate from the truth; for on this account the fable calls him a demigod [34], that it may evince the difference between him and the immutable gods. And the Corybantes [35], who are the three ruling hypostases of the more excellent genera after the gods, were placed round him by the mother of the gods as his guards.

But Attis likewise rules over the lions, who, being allotted a hot and fiery nature, together with the lion, their leader, are indeed, in the first place, the causes of safety to fire; and through the heat and motive energy derived from thence, preserve other natures from decay. Add too, that Attis spreads himself round the heavens, which cover him like a tiara, and tends, as it were, from thence to the earth. And after this manner does the mighty Attis present himself to our view; and from hence the lamentations for his long departure, and concealment, for his vanishings and falling into a cavern, arise. But the time in which his mysteries are performed sufficiently evinces the truth of what I have here advanced: for they say that the sacred tree should be cut down on the very day when the sun arrives at the extremity of the equinoctial arch; that on the following day the sounding of the trumpets should take place; that on the third day the sacred and arcane fertile crop of the god Gallus should be cut down; and that after all this, the hilaria and festive days should succeed.

That this excision therefore, which is so celebrated by many, is nothing more than a repression of infinity, is evident from this ceremony commencing when the mighty sun has arrived at the equinoctial circle, in which place his course receives the greatest circumscription: for that which is equal is bounded, but the unequal is infinite and incapable of being passed over. At this period, therefore, the section of the tree takes place; and after this the remaining ceremonies follow; some of them indeed, through mystic and secret institutions, but others, according to rites which may be divulged to all men. But by the section of the tree, the gods, in my opinion, symbolically teach us that, plucking the most beautiful of productions from the earth, it is necessary to offer virtue in conjunction with piety to the goddess, as a symbol of having lived in a becoming manner in the present state. For a tree indeed germinates from the earth, but hastens, as it were, to shoot up into æther; it is likewise beautiful to behold, affords a cool shade in the heats of summer, sends forth fruits from itself, and liberally bestows them on mankind, through the abundant fertility which it possesses. The sacred institution, therefore, exhorts us, who are naturally celestial plants, though detained on the earth, that collecting together virtue in conjunction with piety from a terrestrial polity, we should eagerly hasten to the primogenial and vivific mother of the gods. But the recalling signal by the sound of a trumpet, which is given to Attis immediately after his castration, is also a signal to us, who, flying from heaven, have fallen upon earth. But after this symbol king Attis stops his infinity through the castration; and the gods by this means exhort us also to cut off the infinity of our nature, and hasten back again to that which is bounded and uniform, and, if possible, to the one itself; after which, when perfectly accomplished, it is proper that the hilaria should succeed. For what can be more joyful, what can be the occasion of greater hilarity, than the soul flying from infinity and generation, and the storms in which it is perpetually involved, and by this means returning to the gods themselves? But Attis being among the number of these, the mother of the gods by no means neglected him in his progressions beyond what was proper, but commanding him to restrain his infinity, converted him to herself.

But let not anyone suspect that all this is said as of things which were once performed or really existed; as if the gods were ignorant what they should fabricate, or had any concerns which it was proper they should correct. For the ancients in interpreting the causes of things which have a perpetual subsistence, or rather in exploring the nature of the gods under the inspiring influence of the gods themselves, when they had discovered the objects of their investigation, concealed them under the veil of incredible fables [36], that through the paradoxical and apparently incongruous nature of the fictions, we might be secretly excited to an enquiry after the truth; an utility which is merely irrational, and which takes place through symbols only, being, in my opinion, sufficient for the simple part of mankind; but to those who are prudentially skilful, an emolument respecting the truth of the gods can then alone take place, when any one inquiring after it, discovers and receives it under the guiding influence of the gods themselves. And such a one, indeed, will be admonished by the ænigmas, that it is necessary to investigate something concerning them; and when he has discovered their signification, will advance through contemplation to the end, and, as it were, summit of the concealed truth; and this not through reverence and faith of a foreign opinion, rather than by the exercise of another energy, which subsists alone according to intellect.

In short, whatever we conceive having a subsistence as far as to the fifth body, I do not mean that which is intelligible only, but likewise these apparent bodies [37], which are of an impassive and divine condition, as far as to these, the pure [38] gods are understood to subsist: but matter eternally proceeded, together with the prolific essence of the gods by whom these inferior natures were produced. And that providence of things, which is eternally consubsistent with the gods, through the superplenal abundance of prolific and demiurgic cause which they possess, and which being seated together with king Jupiter, is the fountain of the intellectual gods;--this divine providence adorns, rectifies, and transfers to a better state, that which is apparently void of life, unprolific, abject, and, as it may be said, the very dregs and sediment of things; and this it accomplishes through that which is last in the gods, and in which all their essences end. For Attis having a tiara ornamented with stars, evidently implies that he establishes, as the beginning of his government, the visible allotments of all the gods in this apparent world. But whatever is sincere and pure in the universe extends as far as to the galaxy: and, as about this place, that which is passive is mingled with the impassive, and matter subsists together with such a mixture; hence a communication with matter is the descent of Attis into a cavern, which, though it did not take place contrary to the will of the gods, and to the mother of the gods, yet it is said to have been contrary to their desire; for the gods naturally subsisting in that which is more excellent, that better condition of being, is by no means willing that they should be drawn down to these degraded concerns; but through the accommodating descent of more excellent beings, these lowest natures also are led back to a mode of subsistence more excellent and more friendly to divinity. Hence the mother of the gods is said not to have pursued Attis with hatred after his castration, but then to have been indignant no longer; but she is said to have been indignant on account of his descent, because, though of a more excellent condition, and a god, yet he gave himself up to an inferior nature. But the goddess repressing the progression of his infinity, and adorning that which was unadorned, through sympathy with the equinoctial circle, where the mighty sun governs the most perfect measure of bounded motion, willingly recalled the god to herself, or rather she retains him perpetually with herself; nor did these particulars ever subsist otherwise than at present, but Attis is always the minister and charioteer of the mother of the gods, and always desires the realms of generation; and lastly, always cuts off infinity through the bounded cause of forms.

Again, when Attis was led back, as it were, from the earth, he is said to have recovered the possession of his ancient sceptres; not that in reality he ever fell from them, or ever will; but he is said to have deserted his dominion, on account of his being mingled with a passive nature [39]. But it is perhaps worth investigating why, since the equinoctial is twofold, we do not celebrate the mysteries of this god when the sun is in Libra, but when he is in Aries; the reason therefore of this is beyond all doubt obvious: for when the sun first approaches to us, then advancing from the equinoctial, and the days increasing, this season, in my opinion, appeared the most convenient of all others for the occasion. And indeed, without having recourse to the reason, which asserts that light is the domestic associate of the gods, I can readily believe that the reductorial rays of the sun are aptly accommodated to those who hasten to be liberated from the realms of generation.

But consider this affair clearly as follows: the sun draws all things from the earth, and calls them upwards with a resuscitating and wonderful heat; separating bodies, as it appears to me, as far as to the most exquisite subtilty, and elevating things which are naturally borne downwards. But all such effects as these are arguments of his unapparent powers: for how is it possible that he, who through corporeal heat can produce such effects in bodies, should not much more draw upwards and lead back again fortunate souls, through an unapparent, perfectly incorporeal, divine, and pure essence established in his rays?

Hence, since it appears that this light is allied to the gods, and to such as hasten to return from whence they fell, and a light of this kind is increased in our world, so that the day is longer than the night, when the royal sun begins to proceed through the ram;--hence, the naturally reductorial power of the rays of the god is shewn by his apparent and unapparent energy, through which a great multitude of souls are led back again, by following the most splendid and eminently solar form of the senses: for the sense of sight is celebrated by the divine Plato [40] as not only lovely and useful for the purposes of life, but as a leader in the acquisition of wisdom. But if I should touch upon that arcane and mystic narration which the Chaldean [41], agitated by divine fury, poured forth about the seven-rayed god, and through which he leads souls back again to the courts of light, I should speak of things unknown, and indeed vehemently so, to the sordid vulgar, though well known to theurgic and blessed men; and therefore I shall be silent respecting such particulars at present.

But, as I before observed, the time appointed by the antients for the celebration of these sacred rites was not irrationally assumed, but with the greatest propriety, and agreeable to the most perfect reason: and an argument for the truth of this may be derived from considering, that the venerable and arcane mysteries of Ceres and Proserpine [42] are celebrated when the sun is in Libra; and this with the greatest propriety; for it is necessary to be again initiated when the solar god is departing from our zone, that we may suffer no molestation from the prevalence of an atheistical and dark power. Hence the Athenians celebrate the mysteries of Ceres twice; the lesser mysteries when the sun is in Aries, and the greater when he is in Libra; through the causes which I have already assigned. But it appears to me that they were called greater and lesser on other accounts, but especially for this reason, because it is more proper to celebrate these mysteries when the god is departing from, than when he is approaching to, our zone. Hence, in the lesser mysteries, the proteleia [43] of initiation take place, and this so far only as is sufficient for the purposes of recollection; as the saving and reductorial god is at this period present. But a little after this, continued lustrations, and the performance of holy ceremonies belonging to the sacred mysteries, succeed: but when the god departs from us to the region of the Antichthones, then the very summit of the mysteries receives its consummation. But see how, as in the mysteries of Gallus, the cause of generation is cut off, so among the Athenians, those who are concerned in the arcana are perfectly holy; and the hierophant who presides over these entirely abstains from all generation, as one to whom a progression into the infinitive by no means belongs, but an essence bounded, and perpetually abiding, contained in one, undecaying and pure. And thus much may suffice respecting particulars of this kind.

It now remains that we investigate the sanctity and lustrations belonging to the mysteries of Gallus and the Mother of the Gods, that if we should find any thing in these pertaining to our hypothesis we may transfer it from thence. But this, in the first place, appears ridiculous to every one, that the sacred law permits in these mysteries the feeding on flesh, but prohibits the use of vegetables; for are not the latter deprived of, but the former endued with, soul? And is not flesh full of blood and many other things which both the sight and the hearing cannot easily endure? Is not this too the greatest argument in favour of vegetables, that injury to no one results from their use; but no one can feed on flesh without the slaughter of animals, the execution of which must necessarily be attended with affliction and pain? Such are the objections which may be raised by many, and those not of the vulgar of mankind: and these very particulars are now derided by the most impious [44]; for, say they, in these rites, the stalks of pot-herbs may be eaten, but the roots must be rejected, as likewise turnips; and again, figs are allowed, but pomegranates and apples are not permitted to be eaten. As I have often heard many murmuring about particulars of this kind, and have myself formerly started the same objections, I alone among all men seem to owe the tribute of thanks to all the gods, but especially to the mother of the gods, not only on account of her beneficence towards me in other affairs, but for her goodness in not neglecting me as one wandering in darkness; but, in the first place, commanding me to cut off, not indeed from my body, but from the irrational impulses and motions of my soul, whatever is considered as superfluous and vain by the intellectual and presiding cause of our souls; and in the next place, establishing in my intellect certain reasons, which are perhaps not perfectly abhorrent from the true and holy science concerning the gods. But my discourse seems to revolve in a circle, as if I had nothing to say on this occasion; this, however, is far from being the case; for in running through the several particulars, I am able to exhibit clear and manifest causes why it is not lawful to feed on those vegetables which the sacred institution prohibits, and this I shall very shortly accomplish; but at present it is better to propose, as it were, certain formula and rules, by following which we may be able to form a judgement of any particulars which, through the haste of composition, may have escaped our attention: and, in the first place, it is necessary briefly to call to mind the account which we have given of Attis and his castration, and the meaning of the symbols which take place after his castration as far as to the hilaria, together with the intention of the sacred lustrations. Attis, then, has been said by us to be a certain cause and divinity who proximately fabricates the material world, and who, descending even to the extremity of things, is at length stopt by the demiurgic motion of the sun, when the solar god arrives at the extreme bounded circumference of the universe, and which, from its effect, is called the equinoctial circle. But we have said that castration is the restraining of infinity, which takes place no otherwise than by a revocation and emersion to a more antient and primary cause; but we consider the elevation of souls as the ultimate design of lustration.

These sacred rites, therefore, do not permit us, in the first place, to feed on seeds which decline towards the earth. for earth is the last of things, into which evil, according to Plato, being impelled, perpetually revolves; and the gods in the Oracles every where denominate it dregs, and continually exhort us to fly from thence. In the first place, therefore, the vivific and providential goddess does not permit us to use aliment which declines towards the earth, but exhorts us to look to heaven, or rather above the heavens themselves. There are some, indeed, who feed on one kind of seed only, that is, on beans, which they consider as not ranking among seeds any more than pot-herbs, since they naturally rise upwards and are straight, and do not drive their roots in the earth, but are rooted in the same manner as the fruit of the ivy depends from the tree, or that of the vine from the reed: on this account therefore, the goddess forbids us to use the seed of plants, but permits us to feed on fruits and pot-herbs; not indeed on such as are almost level with the ground, but on such as are sublimely raised from the earth. In like manner, with respect to turnips, she orders us to abstain from whatever they possess of a terrestrial nature, merely on account of its alliance to earth; but she allows us the use of whatever emerges upwards and raises itself on high, on account of the purity of its nature. Hence, she permits us to use the stalks of pot-herbs, but forbids us to feed on the roots, and especially from such as are nourished in, and sympathize with, the earth.

Again, with respect to the fruits of trees, she prohibits us from corrupting and consuming apples, as being sacred and golden, and images of the rewards attending arcane and telestic labours [45]; and as deserving reverence and respect, on account of their exemplars: but she forbids the use of the pomegranate as being a terrestrial plant; and likewise the fruit of the palm, because, perhaps some one may say, it does not grow in Phrygia, where this sacred institution was first established: but to me, the prohibition seems rather to arise from its being a plant sacred to the sun, and of an undecaying nature, and that on this account it is not assumed in the purifying rites for the nourishment of the body. But after this, we are forbidden to feed on any kind of fish, the reason of which is, a problem in common with us and the Egyptians. But it appears to me, that any one may, with great propriety, always abstain from fish, for two reasons, and especially in purifying ceremonies: In the first place, because it is not proper to feed on things which we sacrifice to the gods; and here, indeed, I shall have no occasion to fear being accused of gluttony, which I recollect was once the case, should any one enquire why we do not frequently sacrifice these to the gods; for we have something to offer in reply to this interrogation. And we sacrifice these, indeed, O blessed man, in certain telestic rites; just as the Romans sacrifice a horse, and, both Greeks and Romans, many other animals and wild beasts, as, for instance, dogs to Hecate: and among other nations, in telestic sacrifices, such like victims are offered, once or twice a year. But this is not the case in the most honoured sacrifices, through which alone we are rendered worthy of entering into communion and banqueting with the gods. Hence, we do not sacrifice fishes in the most venerable rites, because we neither feed on them, nor take any care of their propagation; nor, lastly, have we any herds of fishes, as we have of oxen and sheep; for as these animals are assisted and multiplied through the attention which we pay to them, they are on this account useful to us for other purposes, and for honourable sacrifices to the gods: and this is one reason why I do not think it is proper to feed on fish during the time of the purifying rites.

But the other reason, and which, I think, harmonizes better with what has been before said, is this, that fishes being after a certain manner merged in the profundities of the earth, are more terrestrial than seeds; but he who desires to fly away, and soar sublimely above the air to the very summit of the heavens, will justly abhor every thing of this kind, and will pursue and convert himself to natures tending towards the air, and hastening to arduous sublimities, and, that I may speak in poetical language, beholding the heavens. Again, this sacred institution permits us to feed on birds, a few excepted, which happen to be perfectly sacred; and likewise all quadrupeds which we usually feed on, except the hog: for as this animal is entirely terrestrial in its form, manner of living, and from the very condition of its essence, (as its flesh is excrementitious and gross [46]) on this account it is driven from the sacred feast: for this victim is not undeservedly considered as friendly to the terrestrial gods; since it is an animal which never beholds the heavens, and is not only unwilling, but is naturally incapable of such a survey.

And such are the causes why the divine institution says that it is proper to abstain from certain species of aliment, and which we ourselves understanding, communicate to those who possess a knowledge of the gods. We shall only therefore observe, concerning other particulars, the use of which is permitted, that the sacred institution does not prescribe all things to all; but the divine law, regarding that which is possible to human nature, permits the multitude to use common aliment of this kind; not that we should all of us necessarily equally abstain in all things, (for this perhaps is not easy to be accomplished) but that we should, in the first place, feed on that aliment which the power of the body will readily admit; which, in the second place, we possess the ability of obtaining; and thirdly, to which our will assents. For in sacred rites it is well worth extending the will in such a manner that it may rise above the power of body, and may cheerfully endeavour to comply with the divine institutions; for this, indeed, is eminently conducive to the safety of the soul--to pay a much greater attention to itself, than to the salubrity of the body; and even the body, though in a secret manner, will appear to receive by this means greater and more wonderful advantages: for when the soul gives the whole of herself to the gods, and wholly delivers herself to the guidance of better natures, purifying rites, as it appears to me, succeeding, and prior to these, divine institutions taking the lead, nothing farther now prohibiting and impeding; for all things are contained in the gods, and subsist about them) when this is the case, the divine light will immediately shine upon her. But in consequence of her being thus deified, she transfuses a certain vigorous strength into her connate spirit, which, when included, and, as it were, possessing dominion, becomes through this spirit the cause of safety to the whole body. For that all diseases, or at least the greater part, and the greatest, happen from the mutation and erroneous motion of the spirit, will not, I think, be denied by any physician: for, according to some, all diseases, and according to others, the greater part, and the greatest, and the most difficult to be cured, originate from hence. And indeed the Oracles of the gods testify the truth of these assertions, when they declare, that through purifying ceremonies, not the soul only, but bodies themselves, become worthy of receiving much assistance and health: "for (say they) the mortal vestment of bitter matter will, by this means, be preserved [47]." And this the gods in an exhortatory manner, announce to the most holy of Theurgists.

What therefore now remains for us to say; especially since we have composed this Oration without any respite in a short part of one night, without any previous reading or meditation on the subject, and without even intending to discourse on these particulars, till we called for these note books in order to commit them to writing? The goddess herself is a witness of the truth of my assertion. What then remains for us to accomplish, except recalling the goddess into our memory, together with Minerva and Bacchus, whose festivals the law establishes in these purifying rites? And this indeed took place, in consequence of the authors of these ceremonies perceiving the alliance of Minerva with the mother of the gods, through providential similitude in the essence of each; from perceiving likewise the partial fabrication of Bacchus, which this mighty god receiving from the uniform and stable life of the mighty Jupiter, in consequence of proceeding from him, distributed to all apparent natures; at the same time administering and ruling over every partial fabrication. But it is proper likewise to call to mind, in conjunction with these, Hermes Epaphroditus [48]; for thus is this god denominated by the mystics, who are said to kindle lamps in honour of the wise Attis. Who, therefore, is so dull of apprehension as not to understand that all things which entirely subsist for the sake of generation are called upward through Hermes and Venus [49]? And this recalling power is especially the characteristic of reason; but is not Attis he, who, a little before being imprudent, is now, through his castration, denominated wise? For he was before unwise, because he connected himself with matter, and undertook the government of generation: but he is now wise, because he has adorned with beauty the sordid nature of matter, and has so vanquished its deformity, as to surpass all the imitative art and intelligence of man.

But what will be the end of this discourse? Is it not evident that it should close with a hymn to the mighty goddess!

A mother of gods and men! O assistant and partner in the throne of mighty Jupiter! O fountain of the intellectual gods! O thou whose nature concurs with the uncontaminated essences of intelligibles, and who, receiving a common cause from all intelligibles, dost impart it to intellectual natures! Vivific goddess, Counsel and Providence, and the fabricator of our souls! O thou who didst love the mighty Bacchus, who didst preserve the castrated Attis, and when he had fallen into the cavern of earth, didst again lead him upwards to his pristine abode! O thou who art the leader of every good to the intellectual gods, with which thou dost likewise fill this sensible world, and who dost impart to us all possible good in every thing belonging to our nature! Graciously bestow upon all men felicity, the summit of which is the knowledge of the gods: but especially grant to the Roman people in common, that they may wipe away the stains of their impiety; and that they may be blessed with prosperous fortune, which, in conjunction with them, may govern the empire for many thousands of years. But with respect to myself, may the fruit of my cultivation of thy divinity be the possession of truth in dogmata concerning the gods, perfection in Theurgy, in all the actions which I shall undertake, both political and military, virtue, in conjunction with good fortune; and lastly a departure from the present life without pain, and attended with glory, together with good hope of a progression to thy divinity.

TO THE ANCIENT PLATONIC PHILOSOPHERS

HAIL souls triumphant! Truth is all your own,
Lov'd by the wise, to Folly's sons unknown.
Let Ign'rance proudly boast her tyrant reign,
Her num'rous vot'ries, and her wide domain,
Your wisdom scorn, and with barbaric hand
Spread dire delusion thro' a falling land.
By you inspir'd, the glorious talk be mine,
To rise from Sense, and seek a life divine;
From Phantasy, the soul's Calypso, free,
To fail secure on Life's tempestuous sea,
Led by your doctrines like the Pleiads' light,
With guiding radiance streaming thro' the night,
From mighty Neptune's overwhelming ire,
Back to the, palace of my lawful Sire.

ENDNOTES

[1] See this most important subject more largely discussed in my Introduction to the Parmenides. (p. 3)

[2] For in these all are in each, but not all in all. (p. 6)

[3] For an account of the Intelligible Gods, see my Introduction to the Parmenides. (p. 7)

[4] The first part of this account is already published, and forms a part of one of the notes to my translation of the Cratylus: but the latter part from Proclus on the Cratylus was never before this made public. (p. 8)

[5] i.e. Mercury. (p. 9)

[6] Venus. (p. 9)

[7] Apollo. (p. 9)

[8] That the Platonic reader may be demonstratively convinced that the Sun ranks in the supermundane order of gods, let him attend to the following observations, which belong to the greatest arcana of the ancient theology. Every order of gods commences from a monad, or proximately exempt producing cause: for it is necessary, that every divine cause should be to its progeny what the first cause is to all the divine orders; since it can no otherwise produce in the best manner, than by imitating that which is best. But the first cause in an imparticipable one, or, in other words, is not consubsistent with his progeny; and hence every divine order must have a presubsisting and primary principle of its progression, which, from its similitude to the first cause, is very properly called a monad. The immediate progeny, too, of every divine monad, must be exquisitely allied to the monad Its cause, since the similar, In every well-ordered progression, must

always subsist prior to the dissimilar. This being premised, the reader, who knows scientifically the p. 22 number of the divine orders, may easily collect, that as the ineffable one, who is superior to an intelligible essence, is the monad of first intelligibles, which he illuminates with superessential light; so Phanes, or intelligible intellect, which is the extremity of the intelligible order, is the monad of intellectuals, whom he illuminates with intelligible light. In like manner Jupiter, who is the boundary of the gods, properly called intellectual, is the king or monad of the supermundane gods, whom he illuminates with intellectual light; and consequently the Sun must subsist at the extremity of the supermundane order, must be the monad of the mundane gods, and must illuminate sensible natures with supermundane light: for otherwise the mundane gods would not be suspended from a monad analogous to the other divine orders. And lastly, Bacchus, or the mundane intellect, is the monad of the Titans, or the ultimate artificers of things, whom he Illuminates with light of a mundane characteristic. Hence, Bacchus is the cause of the mundane properties of light, viz. of those properties which are inseparable from a corporeal nature, and which are found to subsist in visible light: for light, as I have elsewhere shewn from Proclus, is an immaterial body.

I only add, that the reader who profoundly understands this theory, may consider himself as possessing the key which easily opens the treasury of the highest Wisdom: but let not any one who has not legitimately studied the philosophy of Plato, deceive himself by supposing that this theory may be understood by barely reading over the above observations; for it is certainly ridiculous in the extreme to imagine that a theory like the preceding, which respects the most sublime objects of speculation, which is the result of the most consummate science, and which depends on a variety of previous disciplines, can be apprehended as soon as mentioned: the man that can entertain an opinion so stupid and arrogant, is not only ignorant in matters of the highest importance, but is even ignorant of his ignorance! (p. 10)

[9] have already shewn in my notes on the Cratylus, that the celebrated seven worlds of the Chaldæans are to be distributed as follows: One empyrean; three ætherial, situated above the inerratic sphere; and

three material, consisting of the inerratic sphere, the seven planets, and the sublunary region. As the Emperor, therefore, In this Hymn informs us that, according to the Assyrians, the sun moves in the middle of these seven worlds, he must consequently revolve in the last of the ætherial worlds. (p. 11)

[10] These lines from Empedocles are as follow in the original:
Ενθα κοτος τε φονος τε, και αλλων εθνεα κηρων, Αυχμησαι τε νοσοι, και σηψιες, εργα τε ρευστα. (p. 12)

[11] For an account of this and the following order of gods, viz. the supermundane, see my Introduction to the Parmenides, and notes on the Cratylus. (p. 12)

[12] See my Introduction to the Timæus for an account of these wholes. (p. 12)

[13] In my Introduction to the Timæus, I have shewn that, according to the ancient Theology, every sphere in the universe is surrounded with a multitude of gods in splendid orbicular bodies analogus to the number of the fixed stars; that these gods are subordinate to the gods of the spheres as being their Satellites; that they are characterized by the properties of the several spheres; and that they are distributed from all the various orders of the gods: so that, for instance, about the sphere of the sun, there is a solar Jupiter, Neptune, Vulcan, etc., and so of the rest. (p. 13)

[14] i.e. In Jupiter. (p. 14)

[15] In Aristot, de Interpretatione. (p. 14)

[16] A reader unskilled in the ancient theology will doubtless imagine from this, that as Homer's chain commences from Jupiter, hence Jupiter is no other than the first cause: to such it is necessary to observe, that Homer's chain, of which Jupiter is the monad or topmost link, is only a part of the whole chain, which commences from the first

cause, as there are various orders of gods superior to Jupiter, the demiurgus of the world. (p. 15)

[17] I have already observed in my account of Apollo and the Sun, in the first part of this Introduction, that though these divinities subsist in wonderful union with each other, yet they likewise inherit a proper distinction and diversity of nature. (p. 17)

[18] i.e. Essence. (p. 17)

[19] i.e. Mercury. (p. 18)

[20] Venus. (p. 18)

[21] Apollo. (p. 18)

[22] To believe that the statues of the gods, such as they were fabricated by the ancients, participated of a divine influence, as much as the substances from which they were composed is capable of admitting, must appear ridiculous to every one who is ignorant that the construction of these statues was the result of the most consummate theological science, and that from their apt resemblance to divine natures they became participants of divine illumination. For, as Sallust well observes, in his treatise On the Gods and the World, (chap. 15) "As the providence of the gods is every where extended, a certain habitude or fitness is all that is requisite in order to receive their beneficent communications. But all habitude is produced through imitation and similitude; and hence temples imitate the heavens, but altars the earth; statues resemble life, and on this account they are similar to animals; and prayers imitate that which is intellectual; but characters, superior ineffable powers; herbs and stones resemble matter; and animals which are sacrificed the irrational life of our souls." Statues therefore, through their habitude or fitness, conjoin the souls of those who pray to them with the gods themselves: and when we view the ancient mode of worshiping images in this light, we shall find it equally as rational as any other mode of conduct in which a certain end is proposed to be obtained by legitimate means.

Some of these statues were called Diopeteis, or such as descended from heaven, "because, (says Jamblichus apud Phot. p. 554) the occult art by which they were fabricated by human hands was inconspicuous." And we are informed by Proclus on Euclid, in his comment on the definition of Figure, "that this occult or theurgic art fashioned some of the resemblances of the gods, by characters, in an ineffable manner; for characters of this kind manifest the unknown powers of the gods: but others it imitated by forms and images; fashioning some of them erect and others sitting; and some similar to a heart, but others spherical; and others it expressed by different figures. And, again, some it fabricated of a simple form, but others it composed from a multitude of forms; and some of these were sacred and venerable, but others domestic, exhibiting the peculiar gentleness of the gods: and some it constructed of a severe aspect; and lastly, attributed to others different symbols, according to the similitude and sympathy pertaining to the gods." Let not the reader, however, confound this scientific worship of the ancients with the filthy piety, as Proclus in his hymn to the Muses justly calls it, of the Catholics: for it is surely one thing to worship the images of those giant-like Barbarians called Saints, and another to reverence the resemblances of divinity; since the former conduct is horridly impious and full of delusion and insanity; but the latter is beautifully pious, is replete with real good, and is divinely wise. (p. 54)

[23] I have already observed, in the Introduction to this volume, that our religious Emperor had not arrived at the most consummate degree of perfection In philosophic attainments, and the present passage proves the truth of my assertion; for, in reality, the lowest forms subsist In the highest, and the highest In the lowest; but with this difference, that the lowest are contained in the highest in a paradigmatical or causal manner, and the highest in the lowest according to ultimate subjection, or after the manner of images. So that all forms subsist in each, but in a manner accommodated to the nature of each; just as earth subsists in heaven celestially, and heaven in earth according to a terrestrial property. (p. 56)

[24] Concerning this fifth body, see my Introduction to the Timæus of Plato. (p. 56)

[25] The original is ενυλων, but should doubtless be αυλων. (p. 57)

[26] The soul is, indeed παμμορφον αγαλμα, an omniform image; and the forms which partial souls like ours contain, are, prior to the Illuminations of science, said to be in capacity, because they are then in a dormant state, and may be compared to beautiful colours secluded from the light. (p. 58)

[27] The, νοερα επιβολη, or application of intellect, which the Emperor mentions in this place, signifies that self-inspective power of intellect by which it is able to pass into immediate contact with ideas superior to such as are participated by soul: and a knowledge of this kind is superior to that of science, above which it is immediately situated. See more concerning this in a note to my translation of the Phædo of Plato. (p. 58)

[28] Nature is that divisible life which subsists about body, which is productive of seeds, and which is the cause to all bodies of vegetation, nutrition, and increase: but this life is void of phantasy, as is evident from its being distributed through every part of the body, and becoming by this means passive in the most eminent degree, whereas the phantasy, which is the summit of the irrational life, is undistributed and impassive. (p. 59)

[29] Forms subsist in Nature fabricative, but not intellective; in partial souls like ours, intellective but not fabricative; and in divine souls and Intellects, both fabricative and intellective. (p. 59)

[30] See more concerning this In my translation of Porphyry's Cave of the Nymphs. (p. 60)

[31] Let the reader carefully remember that Hercules is p. 117 said to have been the son of Jupiter, because, during his subsistence on the earth, he immutably preserved a commanding or ruling life, over

which Jupiter presides, and knew that he descended from Jupiter: and a similar reasoning must be preserved in the characters of the other heroes. (p. 62)

[32] Castration among the gods signifies the prolific progression of secondary divine causes into a subject order. (p. 62)

[33] It must ever be remembered that the gods comprehend and preside over the whole of things in an impassive and immaterial manner. (p. 63)

[34] As Attis is the artificer of things conversant with generation and corruption, he may be called a dæmon with respect to a god who is the artificer of immutable natures: not that he is a dæmon essentially, but only according to analogy; for as it is the employment of essential dæmons to attend on the gods and proximately preside over inferior natures; so each subordinate order of gods, from following the operations of Its proximate superior order, and presiding over subject natures, may be called analogically, dæmoniacal with respect to that order. It is in this sense of the word that Plato, in the Timæus, calls the sublunary gods dæmons in one place, and in another gods of gods; and that in the Banquet he calls Love a mighty dæmon, and in the Phædrus a god. I only add, that the superficial writers on mythology of the present day, from being ignorant of this particular, have dogmatically asserted that Plato only believed in one god, and that he considered all the other powers subordinate to this god, as nothing more than dæmons; but nothing can be more false than such an assertion; for in the p. 120 speech of Diotima in the Banquet, Plato clearly places the genus of dæmons as a medium between gods and men. (p. 63)

[35] The Corybantes form the unpolluted, guardian triad of the supermundane order of gods, and are analogous to the Curetes in the intellectual order. (p. 63)

[36] See more concerning this in my translation of Sallust on the Gods and the World. (p. 65)

[37] i.e. The celestial bodies. (p. 65)

[38] The celestial gods may be called pure with respect to the sublunary gods from the bodies which are their participants; i.e. because a celestial is so much purer than a sublunary body. For as the essences of all the gods are transcendently pure, when one deity is called purer than another, this can only be understood as Implying that the participant suspended from the one is purer than that of the other. (p. 65)

[39] i.e. From his presiding over a passive nature. (p. 67)

[40] In the Timæus. (p. 68)

[41] i.e., Julian the Theurgist. (p. 68)

[42] See my Dissertation on the Eleusinian and Bacchic Mysteries. (p. 68)

[43] The mysteries consisted of three parts τελετη, μυνσις, and εποπτεια i.e. certain perfective rites, initiation, and inspection; and the proteleia, or things previous to perfection, belonged to the two first of these parts, but not to the third. (p. 69)

[44] Meaning the Christians, Epicureans, and perfect Atheists. (p. 69)

[45] He alludes to the Hesperian golden apples which were plucked by Hercules, which formed his last labour, and signify his reaping undefiled advantages through mystic operations; for gold is a symbol of purity. (p. 72)

[46] I have observed that the most vulgar and gross part of mankind are remarkably fond of pork; and this very properly, since like rejoices in like. (p. 73)

[47] This is most probably one of the Chaldæan Oracles, but is not to be found among the fragments of the Zoroastrian Oracles, collected first

by Patricius, and afterwards republished by Stanley. Among these fragments, however, the following Oracle is to be found, which perfectly corresponds in meaning with that quoted by our pious Emperor:

Εκτεινας πυρινον νουν Εργον επ' ευσεβιης, ρευστον και σωμα σαωσεις.

i.e. "By extending a fiery intellect to the work of piety, you will preserve the flowing body." But the Oracle by a fiery intellect, means an intellect full of divine conceptions, and which profoundly beholds the nature of the gods. (p. 74)

[48] That is, beautiful, or graceful, a name which was doubtless given to Hermes from his intimate alliance with Venus; for Mercury forms the summit of the harmonic and elevating, or reductorial supermundane triad, which consists of Mercury, Venus, Apollo. To which we may add, that the Greek word επαφρος Epaphros, signifies one upon whom there is foam; and foam implies, as Proclus on the Cratylus beautifully observes in his account of Venus, purity of nature, prolific light and power, and, as it were, the highest flower of life. (p. 75)

[49] And this because they belong to the supermundane reductorial triad, which elevates through Truth, Beauty, and Harmony (p. 75)

www.ingramcontent.com/pod-product-compliance
Lightning Source LLC
Chambersburg PA
CBHW051551010526
44118CB00022B/2668